I0822897

CITY OF HAMMERS

R. Nikolas Macioci

Cover by Elric DeVault

R. Nikolas Macioci

ISBN: 979-8-218-20389-4

For James Borders, my surrogate son,
with much love and admiration

R. Nikolas Macioci

City of Hammers

For over twenty-five years I collected random words in a cloth bag. All the poems in this collection were created from those blocks of miscellaneous jottings. I literally created each poem from a mostly nonsense chuck of notes. I call them scraps.

"The marble not yet carved can hold the form of
every thought the greatest artist has"

"Every block of stone has a statue inside it and it
is the task of the sculptor to discover it"

"I saw the angel in the marble and carved until I
set him free"

---Michelangelo

R. Nikolas Macioci

An Introduction to **City of Hammers**

"Late afternoon sun tinges piano keys
like smoke-stained fingers. Using
his entire body weight, the first blow collapses
the middle of the keyboard. Chips of ivory splay
in all directions like pieces of white fireworks
or an explosion of fingernails. He beats
the housing until it falls out of place exposing
hammers and strings."

begins the third stanza of R. Nikolas Macioci's poem, "City of Hammers," which shares the title of his gloriously harrowing new collection of 100 poems. The poem's nucleus is Joel, whose fingers bleed after practicing a sonata. During a time when his parents are not home, Joel takes a sledgehammer to the piano:

"At the height of his anger,
he pounds down the row of hammers until
they collapse like dominoes."

Macioci's six sections that constitute *City of Hammers* will detonate your soul, while simultaneously constructing a survivor's kaleidoscope that emits healing and celebration, as his poetry is best at manifesting.

Macioci's artful gems originated as (not so) incidental fragments of thought. He collected random words and poignant phrases in a cloth bag for over a quarter of a century. He began pulling from it superb language chunks simmering for an audience to gratefully consume.

Part one guides the reader into the emotionally overwhelming entanglements of beginning a career as an educator, along with both tender and often brutal and abusive landscapes of childhood. Part two navigates through adulthood, culminating a tillage of regret in "All That We Never Said," which is this section's final poem. The speaker states his epiphany – a desire for a high school friend who once had a newspaper route. With literal, passionate diction, we read "I feel a stir in the back of my mind. I want him/ more than a friend. I want the most possible/ closeness." This is not to be, as the poem tragically concludes: "He joined the paratroopers, and one autumn/afternoon while on maneuvers over Wilmington,/ Ohio, his plane crashed, and the sky delivered him/ to earth like the evening news."

Part three navigates the trappings of caregiving for family members with Alzheimer's and how the speaker becomes more fragmented, losing a sense of self on this journey. We are further hooked into Macioci's vulnerable, language web as part four deftly reveals risk and fulmination: a symphony of shards that simultaneously cut and mollify readers in our engagement.

Part five reminds us literally to breathe even when facing immortality:
"When I had been seriously ill/from a heart attack and dehydration,/ I didn't write poems or breathe poetry/" begins Macioci's "When Poetry Disappears." As the speaker's health rejuvenates, the poem transforms: "With every shift toward recovery, poetry/ surfaced again as my prime consideration."

When readers perceive we cannot possibly ingest more afflicting experiences, Macioci stretches our self-constructed limitations, captivating our senses with an alluring and invigorating final section of humorous poems.

There is no one more adept at crafting poetry, accessible and challenging, than R. Nikolas Macioci. His work is so intimate that it becomes our universal canvas. Somehow, enmeshed in the muck and horror of human despair, readers are released into enlightenment.

Macioci further personalizes his collection by dedicating it to poet James Borders, his former student and dear friend. I, too, share a similar history, having stepped into this venerable poet's classroom nearly 50 years ago.

There is no one more dedicated to the art of poetry than R. Nikolas Macioci who was once awarded Best Teacher in the State of Ohio. As one of his former students, I am forever enthralled with his work as well as the vestige of lessons he embedded in me about burgeoning survival via writing.

Sandra Feen, 2022-2024 Ohio Beat Poet Laureate
Author of *Evidence of Starving*,
Meat and Bone, and
Fragile Capacities: School Poems

R. Nikolas Macioci

Table of Contents

PART ONE

BRITTLE BEGINNING

The principal said my pants fit too tight,
but, in spite of pegged legs, he hired me
because I reminded him of his cousin.
It's 1964. I'm twenty-four and Circleville's
population is 11,059. I'm told upfront
that, as a teacher in the system,
I'm obliged to work at the annual
Pumpkin Show Festival, the event
that put Circleville on the map.

Standing at the window of room 101,
anticipating my first seventh grade class
of the year, I look out at a vista of cornfields,
sweat as if someone has buckled a dog collar
around my neck. Last week, staying
at my aunt's cabin on Big Darby Creek,
I cavorted in cut-off-jeans and no shoes,
wore the same attire three miles into town,
dropped a quarter into the phonebooth
slot, and asked about teaching vacancies.
Now, it was almost time to perform.

Adolescents hadn't deboarded buses yet.
My room still weighed with heavy quiet
until I heard a struggle of bodies enter
at the opposite end of the building.
I wondered if it were too late to jump
into my new Oldsmobile and speed back
to Columbus? I felt as alone as a bleached piece
of driftwood lying in tidal pools of perspiration.
Is the worst outcome that students might toss me
into the cornfield?

They rushed through the door. They weren't
wearing choir robes with halos above heads.
I didn't yet think I had to cast arms skyward
and scream for help. I'll never forget that
beautiful but scary moment when I thought
they are all mine as if they were
a roomful of blank checks on which
I could write any amount of information.

I introduced myself, printed my name
on the chalkboard and called roll.
They answered, and the struggle ended.
I begin to think I'd eaten confidence
for breakfast. I told them they existed
on the verge of new experiences, that
I would lead toward proverbial adulthood.
Pompous? Yes. Naive? Yes again.

After school, I stood at the window once more.
Wearing new skin, I thought about the blank-check
metaphor, hoped I would write them wisely,
not spend a dime too little or too much,
and never have to beg for loose change.

RUINED

From the first row, a student tries to kill me
with a stare. I see anger rise from her
skin as if beneath her skin were miniscule
guns loaded in my direction.   I want
to plunge fingers into my ears, purge
the room of silence that crawls
from a dusty corner. For a moment, I believe
it is I who have killed her with a barrage
of language. Her eyes seem to say
how dare I let fall from my mouth
one word, as if I knew anything
about Emily Dickinson or Walt Whitman.
For a minute or two, she studies
an age spot on my hand, and I think
of Sherwood Anderson's story "Hands."
I pull back, puff my chest out, believe
I am well prepared to teach American Literature,
as prepared as a saint ready for prayer.
This was supposed to be a sharing of souls,
a time when people of mutual interests meet
in a collegiate setting, not a time to tie
each other to the rack. Was she questioning
my style of teaching, the textbook I chose?
I had opened my heart, let pour enthusiasm.
There she sat, a challenging look aimed
like a poisonous arrow at my lesson.
Should one student's attitude matter? Yes.
I picture holding her face in my hands,
beseeching her to know the passion I have
for my subject. Her face would only darken,
menace me deeper. She sniffs as if to say
her nose is more real than I or my poetry.

Corners of my mouth slacken,
I persist, careful as I would be in a poker
game. The bell rings. Defeated, I shut
my folder of lecture notes, slip it into briefcase
dark. I shuffle from the room,
away from her gaze, away from her berating
look that said I am one of the poems in her book
on which she wanted to close the cover.

ASPHALT MEMORIES

In 1950, I could play in the middle
of the intersection of Hinman Avenue
and Sixth Street beneath streetlight
without fear of the occasional car
smashing into me. A motley troop
of us gathered there nightly, mindful
of our fathers' strict curfews.
The intersection became a battlefield
where we played kick the can,
hide and seek.

The leader, a skinny, black boy,
who sometimes smelled of oranges,
shuffled us from one activity to another.
We envied a football hero from Fourth Street
whose log-thick neck made our necks
look like toothpicks. A puffy-faced girl
we called Pinky often drifted into our midst.
The cleanest thing that Jasper owned
was his sweatband. We all knew
about his parents' neglect, but never
mentioned or joked about it. And then
there was the blond, lakeshore boy
whose folks owned a second residence
at Buckeye Lake, and who claimed
he hated being near water except
for his bath. His green eyes glittered
the color of frog skin.

We were words in the text of night,
playing comradeship more than games,
owning a small piece of the neighborhood
and handsful of hunger to win.

SKELETON KEY

The abandoned house loomed within a woods
off Parsons Avenue. Secluded as a monk,
the three-story brick had survived
the Civil War. Cousin Butch and I discovered
the house from listening to friends at school.
Teen-age curiosity outweighed common sense,
so, one summer night, we trespassed.

Butch's fifty-two Chevy bumped down
the long, dirt road leading to the house. Poplar
trees on either side poked holes in black sky.
We dimmed parking lights, ready to explore.

Across a cornfield, a red, radio-tower light, cycled
on-and-off, reflecting in the cupola like a bloody eye
beckoning us to enter. We did, and the house gulped
us into darkness. Cobwebs feathered
our faces, tangled in beams from flashlights.
I followed Butch, and we shuffled from room to room,
audacity challenging nerves. We ended up in the
cupola which retained a mysterious odor
we believed derived from something sinister.

We wound back through the labyrinth
of rooms, fearing something would grab us
from behind, rushed through the main hall,
slammed the great, wooden door shut, but
not before I grabbed the gigantic skeleton key
from the lock.

Lingering on the lawn, we gazed up at the cupola,
convinced we had resurrected something evil.
At that point, we wouldn't have gone back in
for anything. The ghoul that always waits
at the bottom of basement steps was sure to snatch us
if we re-entered.

Sixty-five years later, I still have the key in a small
drawer in a spinet desk along with other keys that don't fit
anywhere anymore.

THE GROVE

A flagstone path led from my grandparents' cottage
at Buckeye Lake into the grove overhung with birches
and maples. The path ended at a rusted pump
with an aluminum cup attached.
Gander, her pet goose, followed each time she trudged
outside.

When I was a boy, I used to wander into the grove.
Its canopied darkness emitting only minimal light
through treetops. It was an eerie place, sinister
and ghostly. Curiosity prodded me to investigate
whenever I became bored with the adults
up the embankment and inside the cottage.

The abandoned chicken coop still smelled
of warm feathers. Grandma always colored
Easter eggs and hid them in the grove,
the chicken coop being one of her favorite
hiding places.

A notched board and two ropes made a swing
between two maples. I used to pull myself onto
the seat, feet dangling, and remember
talk I overheard about grandpa's infidelity.
I didn't yet understand the word, but the sound
of it awakened fear that someday I might lose
grandma's beef-broth gravy, cornbread and dreams.

Loud laughter and talk often rolled down the bank
from the screened-in porch. Someone had dropped
a fishing line into the canal in front of the cottage.
In those moments, I felt caught in a precocious
rehearsal for their eventual deaths, scared, worried
time would take them away like divorce had taken
away my dad.

And so I swung and swung to escape even a hint
of any idea bigger than myself, watched Gander press
tracks into early spring mud, waddle toward me
as if I were his whole world.

BUCKEYE LAKE COTTAGE BASEMENT

As a kid, to use the toilet in my grandparents'
cottage, I had to descend crooked, wooden
stairs to the dirt floor basement. Every step
down terrified me. Picks, plows, and shovels
crusted with chunks of earth leaned against
cobwebbed walls like weary, old men waiting
for my appearance. A rusted sickle, curved
like an eyebrow, dangled from an overhead
support beam. Tools, once used by a stern,
insistent hand lay useless as the dead.
Sometimes, a strip of yellow-brown sunlight
stretched across my feet when I stood
in the center of the large, dugout room
next to the toilet. Often, a child's curiosity
compelled me to take a quick look at those
remnants of my grandpa's past.

On near-tiptoe, when I turned back to the stairs,
away from the one, bare, hanging lightbulb,
fear didn't feel like a complete answer
as to why I didn't want to go down there.
It was the oblique way death was disclosed
that filled my mouth with dryness.

Upstairs again, safe from phantoms,
I would remember how quick my young mind
had turned away from shadowy shapes,
away from a person's life
that had come to a standstill.

THE WOLVES OF ZERO WEATHER

Swags of snow-crusted moonlight
drape evergreens. Sound of our boots
crunch white ground. My uncle slogs
ahead, bolt-action-rifle slung over shoulder.
I am twelve years old and follow
without a weapon or an inclination
to kill. He thinks it time for initiation
into manhood, thinks hunting is part
of the rite. I am spending a week
with my Aunt and Uncle Mohr.
He has spared no exaggeration
of the importance of blood sports,
concludes I spend too much time
alone, reading *those damn books*.

Suddenly, he halts, aims, pulls
the trigger. The shot echoes
through the forest into the deer's
unawareness.

My uncle says *got this one,*
words wolves sing after routine death.
Unable to master his masculine nonchalance
I lag behind, silent.

He stoops, examines his white-tailed catch,
points out where the boiler-room shot entered.
Blood seeps from the buck's heart-lung area.

My uncle ties a short rope around the deer's
neck, tugs, and the deer's legs fold backward
as he drags the carcass home
over snowy, field stubble.

Because I am unable to master this
oversimplification of taking a life,
I do not talk. I shout in my head:
Do you know I shudder
at what you see me seeing?

PIANO LESSONS

Every Saturday afternoon, my ten-year-old
fingers pressed the black, doorbell button
luring Mrs. Dickey into focus behind lace
curtains. Her overbite-smile welcomed
as she ushered me through the entrance
that led to the mahogany bench. She
and I sat so close I could smell coffee
breath as I turned pages to the appropriate
lesson. She would say, "Let's start
with last week's piece." Backbone straight
as a conductor's, curved fingers an inverted
cup, I began to play. She would always
pause briefly for a drink of coffee while
I struggled with such works as Mozart's
Sonata in C Major. K545.

The keys felt cold unlike warmth from her
overweight body beside me. She corrected
mistakes with gentle help that bolstered
confidence. For several years, we had shared
family details. She knew of my broken home,
my alcoholic Dad, abuse that reigned
in my house. Her house guaranteed brief
security. I had memorized her living room
from where the piano dwelled: framed family
photos, scuffed rugs, front-window smudges,
flowered wallpaper. I wanted to stay
in Mrs. Dickey's house forever, and often
lingered longer than the lesson required.
The mahogany bench was a safe place,
Mrs. Dickey's encouragement more important
than notes on a music graph.

When I closed the door, I stood on the wooden
porch an extra minute thinking of my choices.
I could trudge to my dad, drunk, slouched
at the bar in a South-End tavern, or plod
to mom who would buy me a sticky glass of 7UP,
expect me to wait unnoticed beneath the neon
blaze of the Swan Bowling Alley sign
until her team finished. I always knew
I would choose to go to her. She, I suspect,
knew it, too, a pattern that replaced love.
Drinking my soda, I thought about putting
two dollars in my teacher's hand, a reasonable price
to pay for an hour of compassion.

MR. CORDLE'S CORNER-GROCERY STORE, 1950

Sunlight sticks to the glass in the front door,
yellowing it to the color of Easter-basket
cellophane. Inside one long room,
loaves of Wonder Bread dominate
a knee-high shelf in the wooden counter.

My nine-year-old hand grasps a grocery list
printed carefully by mom. I stand still,
hardly know where to step on the newly oiled
floor of plank boards. When I look up
toward the counter, a light from a single
unshaded bulb spreads over the bulldog head
of Mr. Cordle. He faces me as if I were his
hostage, reaches over the counter for my list.

He leans his weight on a ladder slanted
against a wall of shelves. It slides on a track
at the top, passes Wheaties and Cream of Wheat,
comes to an abrupt stop at the blue and orange
boxes of Oxydol. Then, he hoists a broom-like
handle that doesn't have a broom at the end.
Instead, two metal-like fingers magically find
whatever he wants from the highest place
in the store. It seems to me if he could raise
that handle high enough, he could bring down birds
or pieces of sky. I don't ask him to try. I am afraid
to say too much, move back from his furrowed gaze,
worry he will guess my age, hold it against me,
somehow prevent me from claiming the paper sack
he has filled.

I unfold the crumpled five-dollar bill. He hands me change. I open the door, leave his vacant stare behind, hug the sack to my chest, shoulders back with childhood pride.

FLANNEL ROBE

Early evening, Mom melts butter
in a skillet to pop corn. I'm standing
beside her, reach across the stove
for something, and flames, yellow
as old teeth, bite at the sleeve of my robe,
zip up my arm fast as lightning.
I do not have time to cry or cry out
before her hands smother the blaze,
stifle the fire against her own chest.
My nine-year-old mind cannot believe
how fast she yanks the robe
from my shoulders, balls it into the sink.
She runs torrents of water onto the cloth
as if flooding fear away for all time.
I'm stunned still, gape at her head down
at the sink as if letting me know
I never have to question again
how much I matter.

WILKIN'S FIRE

The 1949 Philco radio crackles
"Winter Wonderland." I'm lying
on flowered carpet in front of the console,
propped on one eight-year-old elbow
with a crayon in the other hand.
I hear the words "later on, we'll conspire"
but I think Frank Sinatra is crooning
"later on, Wilkin's fire." Many years later,
as an adult, I realized my mistake.
I've never, however, let go
of my original image because "Wilkins fire"
seemed more interesting than "we'll conspire."
Plus, at eight, I'd never heard of "conspire."
I pictured Wilkins, a farmer on the edge
of acres of corn stubble, heaving wood
onto a bonfire, its bright, yellow flame
burning a hole in the black of an October night.

Seventy years later, I still imagine
Mr. Wilkins tending his fire, sending up
a welcoming blaze. I retained that image
all through the years my mother threatened
to divorce my alcoholic father until
she finally followed through. I retained
that image into young adulthood
when I questioned my sexual orientation.
I retained that image through tumultuous
relationships. I retained that image,
as my skin wrinkled and face drooped.

After all these years, I still see orange fangs
of Wilkin's fire tearing light from the night sky
and Mr. Wilkins, a thin-lipped farmer
with a drooping mustache, stoking my mistake
into perpetual memory.

BROKEN BOY

How carefully my father drank booze.
He was a fastidious, weekend drunk,
triumphant in drowning loneliness.

My parents deserted each other long before
divorce. The child of a disconnected
Mom and Dad, I rotted with guilt,
wanted to fix everything. I forget
the woman's name I caught my father with,
while Mom hid her own version
of desertion.

I felt defeated in my world
of Barthman-Avenue concrete,
trudged streets, alleys, pawed through
other people's trash. The eight-year-old poet
in me salvaged a plastic butterfly
from a rusted barrel, added it to
my collection of talismans to protect
against family uncertainty.
They altered nothing.

My parents couldn't see
how home killed me, catapulted me
into a chasm caused by their separation,
a canyon of discontent that, even as an adult,
I can't climb to the edge of.
It was a hell of a way to raise a child.

EARLY PORNOGRAPHY

My dad made deals with cops,
sold beer on Sunday, contrary to blue laws,
bootlegged fireworks, wrote numbers
with an Al Capone finesse, and hid
a revolver beneath the counter
of our confectionery on Barthman Avenue
in the 1940s and early 50s.

One of the cops, an azure-eyed man,
accompanied Dad on fishing trips,
complimented Mom's looks, and
bought an illegal BB gun
for my ninth birthday.

One night, a week before Christmas,
the cop invited us to visit his house
and meet his wife. When the time
arrived, we slid from our 1950 Ford,
stepped over the threshold and
exchanged amenities.

Shortly after arriving, our host toted
a cardboard box down from upstairs
to share old photographs. The box
stopped on the floor in front of me.
It overflowed with photos as well as
miscellaneous items.

An hour or so later, the adults
had lost interest in pictures. I
snuggled closer to the box. Unable to ignore
curiosity, I felt a sudden urge to dig around
in it, driven by an impulse stark as
incipient lust. The adults formed
a kind of semi-circle, removed from me
by several feet. They didn't appear to see
or sense me measuring when to dip my hand
over the edge on the pretense of looking
for more photos.
The box held keys, assorted papers with
borders brown and yellow as old teeth.
I wiggled my hand deeper, as if
my fingers knew intuitively what I'd find
at the bottom. Holding aside some
of the articles, I glimpsed a booklet
several pages thick. Its title had to do
with a nurse. I couldn't risk staring to read it.
I had seen such a booklet at school.
Aggressive boys had passed it around
to select friends in the school yard.
I had been stirred to hardness.

Looking straight ahead, I slipped
the booklet under my shirt. Though certain
none had seen my crime, I felt awash with guilt,
the tiny bulge under my shirt seemed
as conspicuous as a pregnancy.

Less than an hour later, we left.
I played the lamb at Mom's side, praying
myself from countless apprehensions.

Alone in my room I retrieved the lewd pages,
smothered them with attention, always aware
I'd found the booklet in a cop's house.

THE BELT

It's a humid, July evening in 1949. Lovely
stars the color of snow are everywhere above
the intersection of Hinman Avenue
and Sixth Street. More than a dozen
neighborhood kids have gathered
in the middle of the street to play games.
I am eight-years-old and out after curfew.

Streetlight glints from the buckle of Dad's belt
as he pounds steps towards me from our house
less than a block away. The belt, released
from his waist, dangles in his hand
as much a signal of danger as the warning wink
of Paul Revere's lantern.

I wear shorts, bare legs a target
for drunken rage. I turn to step ahead
of him, but his belt, already mid-air,
wallops, bites my thighs, stings calves.
I have fallen into a nest of wasps. He strikes
again and again, as if to separate skin
from bone. Blood trickles down to ankles.

He prods me toward our house, commands
me up to my room. *I told you to be home*
by dark. Now stop the crying or there's more
where that came from. He slams the bedroom
door, and I hear him tromp downstairs.

I try to hold my breath. I press my hands against
the sill, stare out the window at the two lines
of neighborhood kids, hear the shout
of *Red Rover, Red Rover, send your man over.*

MEAT

The Sunday afternoon I refused to eat meat,
Mom had gone to work in the confectionery
below our apartment on Barthman Avenue.
My dad's shadow, dressed in tyranny,
loomed over my eight-year-old shoulders,
his black hair stuck to his forehead with sweat,
as I stared at the slice of pot roast on my plate.

I had always had a distaste for meat,
managed in the past to swallow a few bites
with Mom in the wings urging me.
Today, gag reflex awaited the first mouthful.
Dad's threats deepened. I pulled a strip away
from a larger chunk, watched the tear of fiber.
He pushed a forkful between my lips into dark
of nausea. Unsatisfied with pretense
of eating, he slapped a burn into my cheek.
I focused on cabinet doors, intent on dark
grain behind which dishes had been stacked
for safety. The sudden tightness of rope
wound around my waist and chest. He stuffed
a dish rag into my mouth. I panicked, cried
to be free.

The under-shirted Dad eventually released me,
warned me to eat and bestow thanks.
I gulped breath, cleared my plate, swallowed
the last bite of beef. Apprehension beaded
with sweat, I asked to be excused from the table,
a stream of sun across kitchen floor
like a yellow path of escape.

THE MUSIC OF NEGLECT

"Caught in that sensual music all neglect
Monuments of unageing intellect"

Sailing to Byzantium
William Butler Yeats

In dim, bar-room light, his eyes glint a hint
of brown. My dad is handsome: black hair,
chiseled profile invite ladies to look.
Whether I sit straight or slump on the stool,
my nine-year-old back aches
from having spent the last hour watching him
down Gambrinus. I'm not interested in playing
pinball, and the jukebox doesn't need my coins
to keep it blasting popular tunes. I am, however,
somewhat mesmerized by colored lights
that trim the jukebox's periphery.
It's a visual escape from the odor of stale beer
and my impatience to leave.

Dad is taking me to the movies this afternoon.
We will catch a bus, ride downtown, but first,
I must endure several stops at bars along our route.
I have finished a second 7UP, am fidgety.
Dad knows many people in this bar. They greet him
with smiles and slaps on his back.
My dad, a generous man, owns a confectionery
on Barthman Avenue, gives more away
than he sells, even though he makes enough
in a week to hand a hundred dollars to mom
each Friday to spend as she wishes.

The South End knows my dad as Shorty.
That name echoes behind us as I slip
from the stool, follow him to our next bar.
He has never said he loves me. I assume
he doesn't, or he wouldn't drag me from bar to bar,
make me wait for a clue that I mean more than
booze.

Finally, we board the bus at twilight. He is groggy,
will sleep during *Vera Cruz,* open mouthed, snoring
beside me.

DAD ON DRUNKEN SUNDAYS

He leans on me as if I were a banister.
We climb stairs through Sunday
afternoon toward a bedroom
in his sister's house where he stays
since his divorce. He slurs directions,
collapses into my shoulder, mumbles
difficult whispers of where he wants to go.
I choke back a scream of frustration
that would, if allowed to scrape
from my throat, scare rats in the walls.
I've been his crutch many times,
deciphered intoxicated mumbling
about how much he misses my mom.

His arms hang at his sides as if broken.
At bedside, I raise his hands to rest
them around my neck while I undress him
and lower him onto the bed.
He always sleeps naked with a burning
cigarette in an ashtray beside him.

I am fourteen and cannot name this
indefinable dance that ends with me
sitting on the floor, back against the wall,
eyes level to his lack of dignity.
Sometimes, he sleeps with his rosary
which I see on the nightstand, coiled
atop a paperback mystery. I reach
for the string of black beads and think
how easy it is to open a drunk's hand.
Saliva dribbles down his chin, swells
the air with stale breath like the bottom
of a day-old beer bottle.

I slouch against the wall again, wait
for him to awaken sober while
the room mocks with his promise
to take me to a matinee movie.

BASEBALL CONFESSION

I find the right bookshelf, SPORTS, trail a finger
along spines, stopping at *Baseball for Dummies*.
I pull the book from the shelf, bend into
a forward stride to the checkout counter.

At home, seated on the edge of my bed,
I open the cover and read all afternoon.
Claw feet of sun grip the carpet at 4:30.
Plum-colored leaves of a maple buck
against the window.

I close the book, thinking how I've glided
through childhood to age fifty
without the vaguest notion of how to play
baseball. I watched Manny Ramirez blast
cowhide beyond the grass line, Omar Vizquel
cup his hand around impossibility and
rocket the ball to first base. My brain burned
with envy.

A fanatical sports fan, my dad, absent
as a spectator at a rained out double header,
never surfaced from alcohol long enough
to teach me the game that would have kept me
from brickbat ridicule at summer camp.

City of Hammers

There, I sneaked away from the diamond,
hid behind a cottage to avoid the moment
when a fly ball might fall into my incompetence.
Behind the cottage, I curled up in fear,
water of the creek near me, sharpening stones,
glittering like the sadness of shame.

I fluff pillows, push my back against them,
envision the day I erase pointless hurt,
enter into major league conversation with men
who seem to have been initiated at birth.

INCIDENTAL SORROW

My dad finally died today
after many self-fabricated attempts
to elicit sympathy from Mom.
He was not suicidal. Drunk,
he invented situations that made
his death seem imminent, fictions that followed
Mom and me into hiding places.
In closets, under tables, we huddled
together, tried to fold into ourselves
and disappear. He always thrust back
into our lives, bloodshot eyes
discovering our faces in the dark.

Although Mom and I wear corsages
of self-congratulations to have survived,
chills of remembrance still stab
our minds like sad icicles
no amount of sun can thaw:

The time a red-haired hooker ripped him
from breast to buttocks with a butcher knife,
his side gaped open like an oversize fish gill.

The night he phoned home from outside Sam's Bar,
claimed he lay in a pool of blood and cheap neon
after someone nearly obliterated his brain
with a blackjack.

The mid-morning crash that flipped his car
and collected his ribs together
like a fistful of kindling.

The Sunday afternoon he smeared toothpaste
on a sofa cushion to corroborate seepage
from a head concussion.

Except for the hooker, his make-believe
incidents should have split his heart in half
with guilt and shame, but, like a liquid bandit,
drinking robbed him of a respectable finish.

Today, his sister called,
and the actual voice of death crawled out
of the phone into my ear, a tame detail
that doesn't touch me anymore.

CAREFUL THANKSGIVING

A carving knife disappears
into a slice of turkey. Ten of us eat
from the polished glint of flatware.
Mom and her sisters constantly babble.
I don't want to be there, upstaged
by a handsome cousin, surrounded
by mundane conversation, so I balance
on a tightrope, rules of decorum
on one side, expression of my true
feelings on the other. Someone
in revolt against varicose veins,
arthritic hands and hand-me-down
values, I kick open a door of leaves,
escape for a walk.

Clouds like gray wolves prowl close
to the ground, pewter sky their prey.
I amble a country road next to a pasture.
Fenceposts, landlords of the field,
catch unexpected snowflakes.
This is the landscape of my grandparents,
he, a farmer who, on foot, herded
a team of cattle from Bainbridge, Ohio
to Columbus. She, a backwood's woman
who had eleven children and barely knew
how to cook beyond burned beans.

Today, at the dinner table, it was as if I ate
the food of ancestors, then disappeared
without a quiver of self-reproach.
Guilt now floods my head because
lineage presses for remembrance,
and I turned away from family for petty
reasons.

When I return, chatter among the gathering
accompanies dessert. Mom asks where I've
been? Skin of her ninety-year-old neck sags
like a limp flag. Knobley hands cover leftovers:
cranberry sauce, mashed potatoes, everything
that passes for an end to obligatory celebration.

THANKSGIVING OUTLAW

Aunt Ada lifts the lid from a bake bowl
brimmed with stuffing. She guards it
as if her secret recipe could be stolen
by inhalation. From a drawer, she chooses
a carving knife, lays its edge against turkey
flesh, slices off a piece shaped like a tulip
pedal. I'm tempted to crack a kitchen window
to dilute a warm November. Outside,
a few maple leaves still hang down
like faded yellow gloves.

I know everyone here and no one.
Aunts, uncles, parents, a brother, brought together
to nibble a crust of pumpkin pie, give
nebulous thanks not ever quite caught in words.

Mom remarks about the abundance of crows
this year. They seem to have fallen from sky
into local fields like pepper
from a profligate shaker.

I slump on a folding chair, assume
all present have speculated about
the absence of a wedding band on my finger.
I have frayed a paper cup, crimped its edges
with my teeth, strangled by hands of convention
on my neck. After all, this is a family event,
a melancholy toast to procreation.

I turn toward Uncle Toots. He jabbers
about Ohio State's unwise choice
to replace a quarterback
with an inexperienced sophomore.
The uncle doesn't know my mind slipped
into a stupor during part of the conversation.
I gather myself back to women
scraping scraps from crusty plates.

Outside, night, a jewel thief, steals last light.
The women pack leftovers, begin farewells
real truth absent from their barren faces.

I drive alone over a bumpy railroad track, past barns
with darkened doors, farm houses with lamplight
yellowing windows. Those at the feast didn't know
I fought a compulsion all day to be away from them,
away from their forced smiles, temporary decorum,
and conversations as insincere as office talk.

BIRTHDAY

Wrapping paper tears from gifts
like something to be rid of. Ribbons coil
to the floor like nervous snakes.
Receiving such attention deserves
correct appreciation, so I'm careful
to thank everyone, yet I feel as if I were
a teacher again collecting mandatory
assignments.

The cake is cut, scarred in front of family.
Slices beautifully smooth give way
under the knife. Those who know
me well know they have failed to satisfy
my emptiness with a bouquet of balloons.
I'm supposed to experience a day better
than summer or one of autumn's moments
when trees display amazing artistry.

Because I question everything, God,
love, and all things about death,
I wanted answers for my birthday.
Nothing is solved with presents
or the congenial sharing of cake.

In my own silent way, I'm grateful
for the celebration. It just seems as if,
each year, I wait for the miraculous gift,
the ultimate one, that will vanish vacant hours
and life's bafflement.

The party ends like a sudden disappointment.
Repetitious sounds of happy birthday and goodbye
echo from the doorway. I put away gifts, wash
silverware, wipe the table, wonder what happens
next. My house is empty now, silent as understanding.
Walls, furniture, gray carpet is all there is in my world.

CLOTHESLINE

I blink at sky, fiery yellow
this time of afternoon as I unpin
laundry flapping in an interment
breeze like flags of surrender.
Clothes have wrapped around themselves,
knotted into cloth cocoons. I release
shirts, towels and pillowcases
from a handful of wooden pins.
I fold each piece before placing it
in a bushel basket, drop pins into a metal can.

It was yesterday the doctor told me
I have diastolic congestive heart failure,
not an uncommon condition, a note
of where I am on the life-death continuum.
He is a young, stocky doctor with a mind
sharp as a March wind. I believe he cares
that I am short of breath.

Bed sheets have also wound around the line,
shrouds with bodies inside thin as rope.
I fold the sheets into compact squares neat
as a finished life. From looking up,
my eyes are sun–numb from glare, the ferocity
of light.

Finished, I place the metal can in the basket
with the laundry, carry it to the back porch,
rest a moment on the swing. I think
how I am at the edge of my life, so conscious
of time. I gaze out over the empty
clothesline, see hawks have returned, occupy
the top of a cellphone tower in the church yard.
They sit there, patient, waiting, their beaks ready
to climb down the air for anything in which
the heart has stopped.

A WALK WHEN IT'S SNOWING

Snow covers the ground today
like a thin, white skin. I'm out for a walk,
shoes kicking up a sugar mist that sparkles
within a late, January aura of sunlight.
As I amble along, my mind fills
with thoughts of recent surgery.
I'm told the operating doctor laid
my heart on a table. Afterwards,
in following nights, I dreamed
blood ran out of my heart and I died.

At home, I showed visiting friends
and relatives my bandaged body,
a long cut down the middle of my chest,
another incision running from ankle bone
to groin. The doctor, awakened from sleep,
performed triple bypass surgery on Easter
morning, giving me a personal resurrection.

I'm steps away from Flower Boutique.
I stop and visit with Chris, the owner,
who asks how I am doing? Many people
sent flowers from her shop when I was
hospitalized. It is beginning to snow
when I say goodbye. Small flakes mean
accumulation.

I head home, thinking about my heart,
the organ that makes everything possible,
hoping there will not be any more scary
moments. Snow is piling up fast, white
as an old-fashioned hospital gown.

A dark-cloud cover has closed off sun.
I am quietly understanding what it means
to be alive again, to make crunching sounds
in snow, to call on a friend, to turn death away
for a little while longer.

BORROWED HANDS

I am too close to my hands when I write,
hands wrinkled as wilted lettuce leaves.
Everything used to be at a distance
such as these old hands. I remember
urgings of youth when I took taunt hands
and youth for granted. I was new bark
on a new elm. Now, if I spread fingers,
I create a momentary glimpse of skin
tightened only at the bone, a lie,
an unbearably sad illusion.

PART TWO

HALLOWEEN SELF BURIAL

I bought a clown suit, tried it on each day
like a prayer. Days in advance of Halloween,
I collected pieces for disguise: red and yellow,
big-toe shoes, painting gloves, long eyelashes,
and a huge, red, bulbous nose.
Couldn't wait to become someone else
even for one night. Excitement stirred in me
each time I climbed in and out of the cheesecloth
costume. Intimate secrets felt hidden, closer
to the bone: playing doctor with neighborhood boys,
beatings from Dad's drunken belt.

When I took off the suit, I felt suffocated. I slipped
it from arms, legs, turned back into a boy
who daily balanced fear and security
on either end of a seesaw.

The special night arrived with rainy streets.
I painted my face geisha-white, cheeks and mouth
ketchup red. I ambled from house to house,
coaxing doors open with greedy threats.
By 9:00 o'clock, I filled with dread
of home, felt something gone because I had spent it.

I undressed in semi darkness, lay the other self back
in its box under the bed, flopped onto the mattress,
my head in shadows. Except for streetlight
through a single window, I wore dark like a hug
of hope, imagined what was left of me
would peel off by morning like a mask, and
someone else would rise out of warm sheets
with confidence that wouldn't crumble.

HOW SAD THE YOUNG LIES HURT

Slumped in a window seat, like a cardboard
facsimile of myself, where sunlight brightens
my wrinkled hands, I can't hide the fact
of being old. It's been a tiresome life
during which I sang songs inwardly,
thinking I was where I belonged, dug deep
and felt less.

My stomach crawls with weariness,
and a surprise of hope would catch me
unprepared for its glitter. How unhappy,
and more foolish than cigarettes,
to want a return to youth, the flesh
unsoiled, the heart free of denials.

I suck in my abdomen as I sit here,
feel a slight ache in my chest like
a knife with a dull edge. Out
the window, a runner, straight
as a javelin, slices through silent
morning, and I think how marvelous
that he can appear to outrun death's
overwhelming finality, the Achilles heel.
If possible, I would be his partner
in that enviable youth, run beside him
at an exclusive distance from demise,
but he has passed the window
and an undercurrent of disillusionment
rises in me, old merely shoved back
for a few seconds until I can feel
that it absolutely isn't there.

FIELD

A cloud door opens, its hinges rusted
with twilight sun. I'm trudging home
from Welch's woods through a field
of cut corn stalks, a stand of distant trees
fast becoming night's phantoms. Snow begins
to fill milkweed pods, catch on other
miscellaneous weeds. I look up, breath
in the air of early stars.

My blood, clean with youth, is hungry
for the hint of moon to become more
than the silver blade of a farmer's scythe.
The snow is accumulating, and so is dark.
In this open field, it feels as if miles
of night enwrap me.

Snowy stubble crackles under foot.
The sound seems to squeeze out of my shoes
with every step. Chill penetrates
my fur-collared coat, and I think how
impersonal cold is. Petty reflections
to keep me warm? I spot my house
at the end of the field. On the other side
of Moler Road, lamplight yellows the front
window.

That night in bed, I layer covers, burrow deep,
think winter is one continuous boot in the heart
the blood remembers even asleep.

LATE IN THE WOODS

I trudge out of Welch's Woods toward home
which is across from a stubbled cornfield.
Surrounding trees form winter constellations,
snow knotted in twisted trunks. Twilight
dims everything that I imagine watches me,
rabbits burrowed deep, warmth from their
own bodies providing fur-lined safety.

It begins to snow. Frozen stars stick
to tree branches. Orange sun, a fiery plane,
lands in sky's dark hanger, its pilot's nostrils
full of the bone odor of cold. My face burns
from the scrape of wind.

When I arrive at my door, I look upward,
hear the sharp echo of renegade geese.
They form a barely discernible V,
air pulling them forward along an invisible path
as if by unseen strings around their necks.

From inside, I look out the living-room window
at dark that has swallowed woods
and the three-hundred-acre field leading to it.
Snow has disappeared too until I turn
on a porch light, everything of earlier
meaning suddenly as gone as the brown geese.

NOTHING MORE

I'm used to the noise of a water pump,
refrigerator, and furnace. They speak
to me intermittently. Nothing more.
Once, however, a squawking bird got in,
and that day will go down as one during
which something talked to me besides four walls
and furniture. I caught the bird in a soft towel,
unlocked the door, let it sing again
to surrounding sky. It would seem easy
to adapt, but I believe more in
the presence of people than in the sobering
seclusion of solitude. Some days, my whole life
is an unmoving painting, a static scene
wherein I am there. Nothing more. Sometimes,
I turn on a spigot to hear water splash
into the sink or open and shut a door to catch
the unmistakable squeak of a hinge in need
of oil. I lower my head against snow
and carry in logs for the fireplace. Blue flames
rise from kindling, pour over the logs
like an embrace of hands. I look behind me.
Was I expecting company, or is it the taunt
of nothing more than shadows?

HISTORY OF THE LAST DAY OF DECEMBER

A trillion breadcrumbs of snow blink
from winter clouds. I slouch at my desk,
an eye on a window and variations
of white dusting a sparrow's wings,
masquerading sidewalks into romantic
pathways. Backyard lawn, tea-bag brown,
accumulates pearl-colored lace.

While I check for mail, a half-baked potato
sputters in the microwave. A late afternoon
shadow lies across the kitchen table
like a silent reminder prompting me to dinner.

It is two-thirds of the way through New Year's
Eve, and I am in conversation with myself
about imaginary hammers, each swing
walling me up alone in this house
with a ninety-three-year-old aunt
whose Alzheimer's pushes me toward
thoughts of suicide. So, I am helpless
to care about the baked potato.

On the window, I see my face reflected
and my marriage to a wasted life.
Someone could look in and spot
the Sony TV, sanded floors, a patch
of loose paint on the ceiling, hollow inside
from undetected moisture, me,
clean from an early bath, looking without
celebration at snow that will soon swarm
beneath porch light, snow that will only
temporarily distract from solitude.

FRIDAY NIGHT AND THE BEAUTY OF UNTAMED ANIMALS

"A Highway populated
only by Untamed animals"
Huck Finn in 1950 (Lighting Out)
by Robert K, Johnson

The Short North, a fashionable,
culture-rich section of Columbus,
buzzes on weekends. Vintage-clothing shops,
upscale restaurants, and contemporary galleries
have brought chic and trendy to a once-derelict
neighborhood. Warehouses converted to bars
cross lines between gay and straight. Electric
excitement of the area puts spiders in the blood.
Even to be on the edge of the crowd exhilarates.

I park my car off the thoroughfare, join
the parade of people on High Street.
Processions of the young go by me.
They are mostly in twos, threes, or more.
They hold hands with music, flashing lights.
Anxious about being old and alone,
I feel like an outsider not worth a human heart.
I could be the grandfather of most
of the passers-by. In the midst of
good-time ruckus, I pull out my cell phone,
as if I'm making the ultimate call home.
My best friend answers, and I tell her
I don't know what I'm doing.
She suggests a movie or going for a pizza.
I thank her, stuff the cell into my pocket,
return to the car, grip the steering wheel
as hard as I can.

PICKUP

We leave the dinner party alone,
separate for appearance's sake,
We squandered time in restless
conversation, losing a bit of a buzz
from many glasses of Merlot.
With no apparent explanation
we let our emotions slide together,
decided to free ourselves of clothes
in the late-night darkness of my room.

You could be wearing a t-shirt
that said "Friday Night Fantasy,"
so ready am I to help you out
of a plain white one. We free words,
say soft sounds for which the mind
doesn't even hope.

Later, you roll from my side.
Streetlight blinds me
with your indestructible brooding.
No more laughs or smiles bubble out
disguised as understanding.
I ask you to leave if the naked act
of honest loneliness punches you
in the gut. You have triumphed.
Your handsome face grumbles,
refuses to humble itself.
You have shamelessly turned
my outcry of urgency to your bite
of silence.

Before you reach the door,
I tell you I've already forgotten
your name, to go and dance
into someone else's solitude
while you're still remembered.

YOU

You cut below the lip,
pull the foil up and twist it off,
place the corkscrew at the center
and turn it. Your indifference
toward me is palpable as rain
without a sky, though outside,
real rain puddles. It is as if you are
gone from the room, your exit cool
but imagined. With dragonfly quickness,
your specter slices into pork roast
with a boning knife, and then
you are back, an actual person
filling our wine glasses with Pinot Noir.

I languish in a chair at dinner,
wondering if you will expose your heart,
mention ennui, say how the end seems
natural and necessary at this point?

After dinner and twenty-five years
of incompatibility, I hit the rural road
along fields where backs of sleek, black
crows catch gray light. I am the scarecrow
hanging by a nail on a post, frightening birds
away from scraps of a dead relationship.
I look out across safe fields, orphaned
from you and the way we had been
laced together.

I will go home, hurt as if with crushed fingers.
Rain will continue to lap windows and mask
the sad sound of a ticking clock. I will clean
the sorrow from my bed and ready it,
should you return unexpectedly.

THE TEASE

I see you undress for the first time
in the useless hope of loving you.
Your skin appears just as I imagined it would,
smooth as a spoon, slightly skimmed with sweat,
each drop a miniature flower reflecting light
of the sun along your back. Buttocks, breasts
your whole bareness looks foreign, made up
of a history of someone else's touches.

Obsessed, I don't even try to move
into contact with your blank, contradictory gaze.
You lie back on the bed, tempting me
while I focus my camera. Noon through the window
tints you the color of cantaloupe and coquette.

I long to appear in the picture with you,
but you have not invited me in or offered
anything except permission to photograph.
You come to me as an aspiring model,
know my penchant for shooting portraits.
We have been neighbors since childhood,
but you do not guess that, in this instance,
I push desire aside to open you softly
with hands of lingering lust.

You have spread yourself before me
like gold for safekeeping. Why would you
bring me to this room as carefully
as you would a bird and suppose I wouldn't hope
for something more than your immoral laughter?

When I reach out, you re-dress and bolt downstairs,
your face dark and sour. I follow, shout apologies,
but know how much I still want to dream
about you afterwards.

THE ACT OF MAKING LOVE IN A CABIN ON NEW YEAR'S EVE

In a log cabin, beside a walnut table
with a tulip vase porcelain lamp,
I kiss her. She lifts her arms and says,
"Oh, God." I pull her up to my height,
wish our world would freeze, keep us
sealed together. Outside, tree limbs
glazed with snow snap against a window.

She zig-zags my shirt from my trousers,
her eyes shining, my body jagged with
chill and lust. She smooths goosebumps
beneath warm hands, whispers the zenith
of desire into my ear as if it were an exit
from winter. Her fingers slide touches
down my rib cage. I stare at a snow-glazed
window across from the fireplace, feel
my heart hammer need throughout
my body. Fiery logs coruscate, light a path
to the bed and shadowy fulfillment.

A JOURNEY AWAY FROM TIRESOME ELEGANCE

The Xerox repairman enters the school.
Students have all boarded buses away
from monotony. I linger in the doorway
of the copy room, thinking if the machine
is repaired soon, I will run tomorrow's test.
He is thirty-fiveish, handsome, tattoos
on the back of his neck. He seems oblivious
of me, so I linger behind him, feel inferior
to his masculine aura. He rummages
through a green, metal toolbox, pulls out
something I can't identify.

I shake off musing, continue to admire
a man half my age whose beefy glance
touches me with a lost look as he wipes inky
hands on a work cloth. He crouches again,
a sexual phantom easing fingers into
the metal belly, his touch crawling deep
within electronic flesh. Warm silence catches
sweat from his wrist. I could say things
before we both are so far apart in one place
fantasy collapses, but I don't.

He scrambles tools away, cleans up his work area.
I clear my brain of self-condemnation
for wanting a stranger's tenderness or even
a one-night scar and a savage morning.

The Xerox repairman nods and smiles
as he passes by me. I place a document
on the copier, press a bottom. The machine
works flawlessly beyond doubt and possibility.

CARPET STRETCHERS

This afternoon, two young men carry furniture
into the kitchen so they can pry up living
room carpet. They fold to their knees, both
men slipping a tack remover beneath the rug.
Lumps and wrinkles have buckled broadloom
into a woven sea of wool waves.

The blonde, blue-eyed fellow grips an edge,
pulls the rug toward baseboard. The other guy,
chestnut hair and smooth-cheeked, waits
to be told what to do next, then pulls slack
toward himself, restoring the carpet
to its proper shape.

Chestnut hair slips tools into a metal box, snaps
the lid shut. The blond hands me an invoice.
They trot outside to a blue van with Richard's
Carpet Service stenciled on the side.
With sunlight glinting from its roof, the van
rolls to the street, disappears in a single turn.

Several minutes after they have gone, I stare
at the carpet, its adjusted surface. For a long
while, I slouch in a green, overstuffed chair,
deeply appreciative of self-assured men
who work together to flatten carpet,
men who sat on their heels to assess the next move
and saw me admiring them. Too timid to touch
their conversation, I flirted with the almost
carnal push of their palms across raised nap
that finally began to hug the floor perfectly.

MAMMOTH HOT SPRINGS, WYOMING

I step to the reservation desk
to confirm a room. Luggage leans against
my leg. I scribble my name on the register,
already see myself captured in a Kodak
snapshot, square chin shaved too close,
smile stretching my face from slack of being
older.

Outside, Rocky Mountains cloud over
with threat of a storm. Lightning slices
twilight. Before I lug suitcases to my room,
I watch rain, like sheets of transparent plastic,
pound lobby windows.

As I unpack, I pretend this is more than vacation.
Perhaps a new life is in the background as much
as the mountains. Worn from travel, I pull back
covers, slip into bed. Tomorrow I will gape
at the thermal area which they say
looks like an inside-out cave.

Morning comes quick, and I dress for breakfast.
I sit at a table facing the same windows where,
yesterday, thunderous rain curtained glass
to untransparent. This early, sunrise is feverish
red with a hint of pink. I look around at other
folks who have come to breakfast, think how
over the years, countless people have disconnected
from daily routines, habits of another world,
to visit here.

The guide arrives, a park ranger fresh
as a nineteen-year-old, dressed in self-assurance.
He talks about limestone rock formations, but
I can't draw my mind away from his youth.
He hinges on beautiful,

July's yellow light glosses tired, expectant faces
that gaze at a broad hillside of calcium carbonate.
Some wear t-shirts on which an Indian praises sky.
Later, many will stop at the souvenir shop
to buy evidence of where they have been.
Back home, they will rearrange whatnot shelves
to accommodate a sunset painted on a cheap ashtray.

AN UNLIKELY ROMANCE IN AUTUMN

On this September day, I stuff canvas gloves
into my back pocket, grip hedge trimmers
and pruners in my left hand. Trimmers,
like silver scorpions, are apt to slice my leg
with the wrong bounce of a hip. In the
right-hand pocket, handles of a pair
of clippers extend like an oversized wishbone.
A black, trash bag in my right hand flaps breeze.

The first task is to prune a hedgerow
that rises toward vein-blue sky. New growth
curves toward the property line,
a perpetual falls frozen in green.
A pocket radio, the size of two parallel sticks
of gum, broadcasts Johnny Mathis
from my shirt pocket. Sun bites
adequate warmth on my neck and arms.

I snap twigs into the trash bag, remember
a moment from yesterday when I stacked dollars
at the cashier's window to retrieve my car
from repair. The attendant smiled a little extra.
I arrived home as if my eyes had brushed against
possibility. She was neat and stylish.
Blond hair, close to her head, glistened
like stream water over rocks in sunlight.

I lift the clippers again, snip more shrubs.
The prefect afternoon lulls me
with warm calm the way only imagined
love can.

CROSSING THE SWISS ALPS

I slouch in a seat on the train to Lucerne.
Across from me a younger man sits stiff
as a nail. He is wearing a gunpowder-black,
heathered suit. He says hello in English
with a heavy, German accent, introduces
himself as Julian His fingernails
are trimmed and clean. He is traveling
to Kriens to visit his ailing mother whose
cancer worsens each day. If he were
a smoker, I could see match light bully
the dark and reveal hazel eyes. He says
she has not finished what she can of love
before her flesh hurries to kill her.
She is fifty-two. Strange words
from a stranger, but I accept his trust.

Outside the train window, December sky
is gray as tin, and a small plane skywrites
icy scratches. Staring through glass, I
watch pieces of landscape cut into memory.
Trees, mountains, and houses smear by
as if from one continuous brush stroke.

Julian has become silent. We listen
to the continuous click and clack of wheels
over steel tracks, a monotonous lullaby.

Dark comes fast and cold as the moon
climbs like a bracelet around the wrist
of night. Julian says the moon is a yellow
trinket, a life-size child's toy. I comment
on how poetic his words are. He says
he writes poetry, none ever published.

The train burns space as the engine speeds
through forest after forest as if the locomotive
were a hunter stalking prey. When we pull
into Kriens' station Julian rises.
The power of my attraction to him escapes
through our handshake. His goodbye
sobers me to stamp out the sting of infatuation.

MEETING A STRANGER AT A DINNER PARTY

One Saturday night, six people met for dinner:
two couples, a stranger and myself. The handsome
stranger's hazel eyes caught my glance
several times. His chestnut hair gleamed with gold
highlights. I donned a mask of non-nonchalance,
so he wouldn't guess my instant attraction to him.
The four others chattered non-stop, while the quiet
between the stranger and me became awkward.

Ironically, at dinner, the stranger, Sam, and I
sat across from one another sipping Merlot
and consuming cheese-stuffed dates,
herb-rubbed pork tenderloin, and toss salad.
We looked at each other hard, and I wanted
to sputter intellectual conversation. Instead,
a surge of mindless confidence flew from my mouth
in the form of get-to-know-you clichés. He responded
with polite answers about his work as a lineman
for American Electric Power. Though not completely
relaxed, I felt less alienated from Sam by silence.

After dinner, I yielded to the majority and played
a game of Loaded Questions. I wanted to stop and resume
my conversation with Sam. I had no idea how he felt
about me, but timid and careful as a man on a tightrope,
I didn't want to fail at love again because of impetuous
feelings. In this setting, on this occasion,
there were rules to how far I could satisfy curiosity.

The game ended, repartee and word dance over.
We were all in winter coats, standing on the front porch,
November sky dark but for a slice of salt-colored moon.
Goodbye hugs exchanged, Sam's didn't linger,
an innocent farewell, a brief, polite touch.
Yet, it hurt to pull away, clumsy to hold longer
than the limit of decency and decorum permitted.

As he walked to his car, streetlight accentuated
the gold strands in his hair. I stopped at the door
of my car, watched until he disappeared
along with the wonderful something
I only imagined.

BOOKSTORE

Two young men enter, and nothing can save me
from being stunned by their beauty.
Their anonymous jawlines are tight, defined
as if newly sculpted. I scuttle behind a rack
of bestsellers to hide my age which is at least
six generations older. I thumb through a book,
my mind indifferent to the words, and steal glances
when I think I can without being caught.
They have ambled one row over from me,
and I catch glimpses of them through spaces
between shelves. I want to hide my sagging
skin and eyes. Even my blood feels ruined
by age.

Before I realize it, they slip into my aisle,
peruse shelves as if looking for a particular title.
I want my body to disappear, belly and all.
I shut the book, saunter to the door, wanting
to write my emotions down rather than buy
what someone else has already written.

As I amble to my car, I can still see their short,
black hair, slim throats, how they huddled close
to examine books. Had I even been on the rim
of their sight, or immediately dismissed
as the old guy? Are they coy twins?
Perhaps they've struck a marriage deal
between them, something that would jail a boy
in my day. Maybe they at least sleep within
each other's kindness but joke about men like me.

In the rearview mirror, I catch them coming out
of the store. They look in my direction, or
so it seems, and then they flicker out of sight.
A shaft of sun flashes through the windshield,
pours over me like a touch of freedom
as I wheel away from the curb.

ALL THAT WE NEVER SAID

Jim, my high school friend, reclines on the lawn,
rolls newspapers for his four 'o clock route.
I like watching. It's a quiet, July afternoon.
Mosquitoes, close as a bad dream, pester my head,
distract me from staring at his perfect neck, skin
taunt with youth. He brings a paper to his chest,
rolls it around itself, tucks both ends to stop the paper
from unfolding. Many afternoons I have watched
this routine as we shared school trivia and lamented
about girlfriends we didn't have but wanted.

This afternoon is different. As I follow his eyes,
study his hands repeating the folding sequence,
I feel a stir in the back of my mind. I want him
more than a friend. I want the most possible
closeness.

He finishes preparing, and, often, like today,
I trudge along with him as he flings papers
onto porches. Sometimes, I hang back a little
to memorize his confident gait. Sometimes,
we jump onto his blue Schwinn, and I hold
tight to the metal ring that encircles the seat,
knowing not to touch him.

Finished delivering, we return to his house,
stack records onto the fat cylinder
of an RCA 45 player in his bedroom.
The soundtrack from *Giant* blasts from the speaker.
His bedroom is small. We sit close.

I remember all of this from a long time ago.
More than sixty years have passed since
he found a map out of adolescence, thundered
into manhood miles from his front lawn.
He joined the paratroopers, and one autumn
afternoon while on maneuvers over Wilmington,
Ohio, his plane crashed, and the sky delivered him
to earth like the evening news.

PART THREE

THE ALZHEIMER'S HOUSE

Aunt Liz's arms are sticks, the kind poked
into a snowman. Her body, frail
as sickness, yet tough as two beers
a day, wanders toward me in the kitchen.

She teeters as if supported only by summer
light through a window above the sink.
Her wrinkled face sags,
a ninety-three-year-old mask of slack skin.

The doctor says be kind, be positive.
Day after day, I offer affectionate pats
and words that soothe the disoriented
uncoiling of her brain.

Aunt Liz blunders a step toward me.
I have just finished drying a skillet
and several forks. Her tiny stance
invites me forward into a hug.
A hug is part of the language we use
to speak to each other and to plumb
the deep sleep of her memory. I hold
her bony frame against me, make
a safe place for both of us. Contact stops
nonsense words, her lapse into paranoid
thoughts that spies in a telephone booth
across the street watch us.

I hold her, walk fingers down her back
until all doubt is gone that I am there.
Her life has been minimized
to self-administered eye drops twice a day
and a toilet lasting past noon.

Pulling slightly away, I notice tomatoes spots
dribbled onto her clean blouse during lunch.
I assess the moment, wonder which of us
needs embraced the most.

A LIFE I HAVE MISSED

Snow, like an explosion of swans,
swirled over storage boxes I carried
from my Ford Capri into Aunt Liz's
house. She said I belonged there
because she was childless, and
I would someday be her sole benefactor.

The day I moved in, I swung clothes
hangers of suits and jackets over my shoulder,
relieved to find a place so welcoming.
I didn't foresee that I would have to give up
the choice to come in late from work, to play
music I preferred, to sit on the other side
of a bedroom door without guilt of neglect.

Since that day, twenty-three years ago,
responsibilities for her welfare
spilled into my life like a fountain's overflow.
I lost afternoons when I could sit alone
on a cedar chest, gaze out a window,
content with my own company.
Her dominance, like a feral cat,
hunkered, ready to claim my whereabouts
by the throat.

If I escaped to the yard to assess how tall
the grass had grown, she appeared
at a window to locate me,
so I made myself invisible
by smearing my face with shadow
of a maple, afraid if I moved
into view, I'd be beckoned back
into the house by her Alzheimer's.

THE DANGER OF EXTREME AFFECTION

I escape down basement steps
with the excuse of pressing a week's worth
of work shirts.

The iron is ready when an orange light
on the handle turns off. I press a button,
and steam fans out from the sole plate,
hiss seeming to emanate from my hand.
I pass the iron over cloth, renew each shirt,

Finished, I pull a short chain
on an overhead bulb, start upstairs, reluctant
to relinquish a reprieve from Aunt Liz's
Alzheimer's.

She meets me in the kitchen, happy
that I ascend and have not run away.
She fills a glass with water
she will carry to bed and sip
throughout the night. I engage the alarm
system as if burglary were imminent,
tell her what I have done in the basement.
She slips into my caress.
A ninety-three-year-old woman afraid
of finality, sags against my chest.
Bony shoulders and hips stab me.
I shift slightly away.
She follows a step or two.

I enter my bedroom, close the door,
slide the security bolt into place.
Staring at the bookcase, I imagine someone
who has freedom to have a lover instead
of handing his life over to a book
on a bedside table.

FORFEITING ANOTHER INDIAN SUMMER ON FREBIS AVENUE

Aunt Liz's arm in mine, we amble
around the backyard periphery.
The day is ripe with pumpkin-orange sunset.
Gold eloquence of light has begun to die
within cedar branches. She bumbles
Alzheimer's steps over uneven ground.

Her ninety-three-year-old eyes sight
a ladybug-like beetle on an oak leaf.
She stares at it as if transfixed,
comments that a magnolia tree
has doubled in size since she last saw it
yesterday from the kitchen window.
We stop within a sprig of shadow
from a pine tree. Silence hangs
between us as we cool from warmth
of late October. A crow alights,
pecks lawn for a beakful of something
mysterious that will satisfy
its hungry jitters.

She claims my forearm, and we shuffle
toward back-porch steps past dirty
clotheslines. Months ago, she commanded me
not to expose our wash to contaminants
sprayed each day by foreigners whose mission
is to steal the very air we breathe.

I release her for a few seconds, reach
into my pocket for the garage door opener.
The door squeaks up like a metal jeer.
She squeezes steps forward, and I follow,
glance at rose bushes pruned for winter,
push aside greed to shut myself into my car
and drive away. At the living room window,
her silhouette swims up the glass.
I enter the garage, a box-like coffin, hear whirring
of flies caught in a spider's inventory.

THE ONLY EMBRACE

I stare at my hand, wrinkled as Aunt Liz's,
think about years of monotony and caregiving,
planting tomato plants in her futile gardens,
of watching rain-soaked buds pop open
pink as infants on the same dogwood trees
each spring. I have perfected obedience,
disappeared into the nephew
who lubricates Aunt Liz's glaucoma
with Xalatan, cooks facsimiles of meals
she once prepared. On warm days, she loops
her arm through mine, and we amble
the half-acre backyard, each step a risk
to her balance. Yes, I am a disciple of family,
taught to park my car in the garage after college
and stay put.

At this moment, I am slumped
at the kitchen window, February
lawn finally unlocked from snow,
her finch feeder filled with sunlight and the blur
of wings like applause for seed I have replenished.

Aunt Liz suddenly appears beside me.
No matter how many times this happens,
my body is never ready to accept interruption
of momentary solitude I've eked out for myself.
She slips one arm and then the other around
my shoulders, an act of affection
she had never been unable to show until Alzheimer's
set in. The close puff of her white hair
smells like a warm-woolen blanket.
I turn and see a squirrel squatted on the windowsill,
Aunt Liz puts her head on my chest,
and the squirrel watches as if it were witness to a truth
that in my late age, I may never be held by anyone else.

DEGRADATION

I'm made of absences:
the absence of listening to music
in the main part of the house, absence
of a head on the pillow next to mine,
absence of privacy that guarantees
my mail won't be opened by anyone
but me. Each day, Aunt Liz's Alzheimer's
lays a nonsense path before me
like a garden row of confused seeds
she doesn't know she planted.

Aunt Liz and I exist in an airless house
in which I sniff to detect a burnt pan
on the gas stove, pause to determine
if a faucet runs unattended.

At six a.m. in the morning,
I step onto the floor, tangle in the bars
of my cage as I hunt a sock, tie a shoe,
wipe a washcloth over my face.

In the kitchen, she balances a cup
of tea, spills it crossing to a recliner,
concave to accommodate a body old
as a knee-length bathing suit.

All day, I bow to subservience,
wash her back while she holds a towel
across her breasts, clean up her attempt
to make bean soup when the loose lid

of a pressure cooker blows beans to the ceiling.
I heave the fifty-year-old, iron stove away
from the wall, scoop beans into a saucepan,
scrub walls, floor, sides of cabinets.

Sun lapses to four 'o clock, and she wants
finger and toenails filed.
She inherited Nail-patella syndrome.
Her nails resemble wooden fragments
embedded on the ends of fingers
and toes. Nail slivers angle upward,
edges sharp as pinpoints.
Although the nails defy a file, I succeed
in leveling them to a smooth tolerance.

When night comes, she follows
a well-worn trajectory, turns lamplight off,
removes false teeth, settles in bed
with a glass of water on the nightstand.
She sips water during the night
as if it were an elixir for longevity.

I turn a key in the back door.
The porch overflows with cream-colored
moonlight. Star ornaments have been
hooked to the sky. For the first time
all day, I feel free, step from porch to hose
lying in overlapped circles
next to the sidewalk. I turn the faucet on,
pull the hose to a grassless patch of earth.
On knees, I work sodden soil
into mud, comb it through fingers,
shoulders drooped in resolve.
Mud sticks to hands, cakes under nails.
Finished, I flatten a piece of mix
into a palm-size glob,
place it on my tongue and swallow.
Shock of ingestion passes, the taste
in my mouth, deserved punishment
for the life in which I have trapped himself.

SNOW HANDS

Each snowflake, a white, lacy hole
in the air, a winter blossom falling
from a tree of sky, accumulates
on the driveway. I stare out
of the living room window
at weather turning landscape
into a bride's gown.

Behind me, Aunt Liz drops into a sunken
recliner. Her body slackens to a slump,
mired in the quicksand of Alzheimer's.
I sense her rodent eyes gazing at my back,
as if they were voodoo dolls stabbing me
with demands. I turn to see her
ninety-three year-old face smudged with
too much rouge, lipstick slightly above
her upper lip. She bends forward, squinting,
like a woman with hammer in hand, ready
to pound truth into my head, says, "No need
to shovel. It will melt." I step to the window
again, see moon-colored boxwood bushes
in terraces below me. I almost topple
an antique lamp as I hurry for coat, gloves,
and cap from the hallway closet.

Escaped to the garage, I press a button,
and the garage door squeaks upward,
opening to a modicum of freedom.

When I step out, feet sink in a foot of vanilla
fluff. I thrust the shovel deep, lift it full
as possible, repeat this again and again,
as if it were a mantra that could change
everything in the house.

For the moment, snow has become a scattering
of flakes. I continue to pile shovelful after
shovelful, toward where sun should be.
Satisfied with my progress. I take a breather,
look down, spot a large rock at the side
of the driveway. I scoop up a handful of snow,
pack it around the rock, crook my arm, ready
to catapult the snowball through the front window
to shatter her disease and my pent-up emotions.
Instead, I drop the snowball, lock eyes with her
watching me, shackled by commitment
and the responsibility of winter.

IN THE BASEMENT

I slip into a moment alone,
sweet as wisdom itself. Sunlight,
yellow-gold like an elm leaf in October,
pushes through a dirty window, streams across
concrete floor, dilutes late-afternoon dark
that hangs from rafters like shadowy bats.

I slouch in the workbench chair,
assorted tools to my right hooked to pegboard.
This is where I escape when air upstairs turns
brittle with Alzheimer's. Aunt Liz, ninety-three,
circles rooms again and again. She doesn't
know she is rowing a sinking boat of recovery
nor understands the mast has fallen, crushed me
temporarily into this makeshift chair.

I focus on furnace ducts as if I had
a tenderness for metal, pin sight
to the cold facts of things: a worn, braided rug,
a ripped, overstuffed chair, an ironing board.
I want to fuse with these things, be absorbed
by them, but I bide my time as if I were
in a foxhole waiting to be shot.

She scoots steps above me. Dust sifts down
from between rafters. Sunlight continues
to bend through the window. I have devoured
my break away from her, must ascend, tumble
back into routine, monitor every moment.

She's at a front window. It's time to apply
makeup on her slack, stoic face. Her sister
will arrive soon to pick her up.
What I really want to do is push a knife
into my stomach, spill out all the loneliness.
I help her into her coat, pull it over shoulders
of canceled grace, grasp a curtain cord,
shut out drivers whose glances cloud her
mind with fear and paranoia.

CRUEL INTERLUDE

Dementia, bane of Aunt Liz's brain,
settles down like a vulture on a limb,
awaiting her next response. She props
her back against the corner
of the zebra-pattern couch, TV
light flickering across her
ninety-three-year-old face. Late
on a Sunday evening, she holds a cup
of warm whiskey, lemon, and honey,
steadies the cup against her shriveled lips,
draws comfort over the porcelain edge.

It is early March, and she has survived
another winter, wrapped away from cold
in secondhand quilts, awaiting green of spring
she says seems as distant as another planet.
Her head droops to her chest, drifting off
as if rehearsing a conclusion, then
her head rolls upward, surprised
to see light again.

All of this I observe when I slip past her
on a path leading to the bathroom.
Before I return to bed, I study her
from dark of the bathroom doorway.
I am frightened to think this is what
she has left of life, to come awake
intermittently, to be who she once was
only at intervals.

THE CAREGIVER'S MESSAGE

I pluck hair from Aunt Liz's chin,
aim an eyebrow pencil at a hint
of eyebrow and sketch in brown lines.
Aquanet locks a halo of white hair
in place. I select a blue, Liz Claiborne
blouse. From a plastic compact, I drag
a sponge across Revlon's Original Rose,
feather rouge onto her cheeks,
soften the effect with light strokes
of a folded tissue. I tie her Easy Spirit
shoes, check buttons, make sure
the top one is shut against immodesty.
I apply Flame Red lipstick bright
as blood on snow. Finally, she is ready,
lounges in a recliner, waiting
for my parents to pick her up.
I leave her with late-afternoon sun falling
upon hands folded across stomach,
open the basement door and descend.

Separated from her Alzheimer's, I pull
the cardboard box, in which a new hot
water tank arrived two weeks ago,
from against a wall, lay the box parallel
to the floor. I open the flaps, step over
the side, lie down, and pull the flaps shut.
I fold arms across my chest in the traditional
pose of a person in a casket. I do not grasp
the ankle of God to save me, but soften into
the idea of death. I feel my chest rise, fall.
I hear the latch on the front door unlock,
confident she is still able to find her way
to my parents' car, a frequent routine.
I imagine the car slowly moving down
the driveway, bird flutterings of light pattern
the window and her stoic face. My burial ends.
For a few hours, I am unchained from duty.

MONDAY EXIT

I slide my arm around Aunt Liz's waist
to support her. We don't speak, but dwindle
away from her chair toward the bedroom.
Even before we reach her bed, I know
she is finished walking, forever.

I lower her onto the mattress, wondering
what actor stole her identity and is now
playing the part of a woman with only a body,
Alzheimer's having taken away her tongue.
I snap on a bedside lamp. A circle of saffron
light reveals a sofa, dresser, and nightstand,
a tableau of somber solitude.

For three days, she has moaned of feeling sick,
gone without bowel and urinary relief.
With reluctance, family concedes the time
has come for emergency help.

The squad slips up the driveway
quiet as tenderness. Four young men
and a woman, all with ruddy cheeks,
as if they had just returned from a sunny beach,
begin the mechanics of life-saving, reduce it
to an impersonal pantomime of five shadows
in a choreographed dance. Ultimately, they
make a hammock of her bed sheet, fold her away
from my eyes.

The paramedics gurney her into the squad,
and I'm invited to accompany. The siren rips
holes in the night, as we race through red lights,
bounce forward. During this ride, I remember
the light in her bedroom still burning
across the remaining white sheet
as if having been snowed upon.

PRETTY PEOPLE IN THE HOSPITAL

I'm more afraid of doctors and nurses passing me
from one mistake to another then I am of
impersonal computers that don't rank me
in a pecking order according to looks.

Studies have shown over and over that appearance
counts when it comes to privilege in hiring
and hospitals. Although, sometimes, a positive
personality can override being old or unattractive.

Hospital staff hold the path to eternity in their hands.
Workers manipulate wires, test tubes, machines,
listen to patients' prayers in midnight whispers
or during drugged seconds before dying.

Three nights, I slumped in a chair beside Aunt Liz's
hospital bed. Her ninety-three-year-old hands reached
out for healing. Skin sagged along arms, draped
from bones like the cloth of a shroud. She lay soft,
disgusting for the young to touch.

Although reluctant, they attempted to provide comfort
while their faces shouted *thank God for youth.*
They seemed squeamish about oldness
they did not understand.

The competition to be cared for is tough,
the wait, interminable for a minute of a stranger's time.

INEVITABLE PORTRAIT

I watch rain distort Aunt Liz's
reflection as cellophane lines of water
roll down hospital windows.
I turn back, lock eyes with the nurse
who has named sound emanating
from the bed as agonal breathing.

Aunt Liz's hair, smashed into the pillow,
fans outward, blurring a recent permanent.
Her open mouth gasps for air.
Three remaining teeth push her lower lip
forward. I recall her story of how childhood
poverty robbed her of dental care.

I turn off fluorescent light behind the bed.
A secondary light glows soft. The sky
is not a part of this, but I turn to the window
again, stare at rain scribbling the glass.

The whole world slides by
on wet streets below, oblivious
of me waiting for the abrupt second when
this room has nothing left to offer.

Half a glass of water on the bedside table
reflects light from the hallway. I lean
forward on the edge of a chair, flex my back,
aware of every second draining from her.

I am thinking of how much she loved
Fig Newtons when her chest stops
even the least perceptible movement.
Even though I realize it doesn't matter
anymore, I reach down and push the button
to bring a nurse. My finger is still on the button
when the nurse slips through the doorway
and hugs me, a practiced embrace
she has been trained to do at the end.

END

Death, the architect of decay, claimed her
at 3:30 on Sunday afternoon.
The flowering light of April stunned
hospital windows, silvery as the days
before she lost hope.

I know she was looking for much more life
than she got, but found she was only going
to be released from the failing of her body.

For days, she wrestled with delirium,
a kind of battered ecstasy.
Each hour, her breath became less visible
and then non-existent.

Early this morning, I took her hands in mine,
and though we did a kind of motionless dance,
I knew she wanted to kick her heels up and soar
away from the beautiful sleep that is louder than life.

AFTER AUNT LIZ'S DEATH

Stoop-shouldered, I shuffle from room to room,
note doorknobs, unpolished floors, infinite
silences where words used to be. Alone now,
I raise eyes to your absence. Chairs, tables,
and the dust of my life will only move
if I move them. Your aging face accompanies
me everywhere. At night, when I lie down
on the bed, a lifetime of memories swallow me.

I imagine I understand death, but I don't.
I understand only what I have lost. Through
remembrance, a left-over gift of the mind,
I see sweat of your daily work, your patience
with monotony, our friendship that understood
without saying anything.

Eventually, I will adjust to your absence,
continue to search corners, squint to see,
as far as the room will allow, any signs
of you. Of course, you won't be there, and
I'll accept the nothing I find, while I look
for the impossible, my heart raw and bare.

AUNT ADA'S APPLES

Aunt Ada thought apples could fix the world
for a while. Daily, she watched out her kitchen
window as countless buds blossomed
into tissue-thin flowers on a webwork
of branches against sapphire, summer sky.

Eventually, clusters of Melrose apples ripened
into a ruby-red blush. Sometimes, she would
pile them into a basket or make a quasi basket
of her apron. Like perfect prizes, she floated
them in a flood of hot, sink water. Then,
she peeled each one with a gleaming paring knife,
rind unwrapping in one continuous strip, dropping
onto newspaper spread on the floor to catch them
as they snaked into a pile.

When she had accumulated a mound of slices,
she rolled dough to create pies and dumplings.
She repeated this sequence until the apples
at the top of the tree were too high to reach.

For weeks, aroma of spiced heat curled
from the stove, a trace of it in every room.
For weeks, apples bobbed to the brim
of the sink. She ended the season having
baked and frozen forty pies. She said
the reason she worked so hard at it
was to share. She supplied friends and family
with these baked confections for as long
as she could obtain apples.

She risked reaching for apples through
yellow streaks of bees, aggravated
varicose veins standing beneath the tree
and for hours at the sink. She believed
the apples were gold and could fill
an empty space like gifts from the heart.

AUTUMN AND EXACTITUDE

I have always thought leaves can kill.
Like bad renegades breaking from maple,
they flood the windshield, orangish-red
foliage sticks under the wipers. I slouch
in the backseat of Mom's 52 Mercury.

I am eleven-years-old and don't yet know
the real truth about how leaves twist themselves
from trees, so I pull my arms in close
to my stomach, imagine the invasion
of greenish-yellow saucers like the ones
in the movie, *War of the Worlds*, I saw
at a Saturday matinee.

We cruise at ten miles per hour
through Laurelville toward Aunt Mary's cabin
in the Hocking Hills. Mom instructs
Aunt Mary about the right way to cook a roast
and the lack of ambition among the young.
I am at a loss to know how to tell them
we are defeated which doesn't mean that roasts
and work aren't important, but leaves are following
us, a gold and brown river behind our car.
How can I tell them the rainbow
of trees arching over gravel byways,
like two hands trying to touch,
will soon siphon our identities
and stamp our foreheads with sycamore and oak?

We stop at a rural grocery,
scarlet leaves clustered beneath tires,
purple sumac sticking to our shoes.
A Burger sign flashes welcome.

Inside the store, I ask for bubble gum
and a comic book. Mom opens her purse.
I lean elbows on the counter, think I hear
a spaceship hovering in October dusk,
waiting to rocket us away from
the inundation of autumn decay.

PHOTOGRAPH OF THE MOHR GIRLS

Seven sisters and their mother stand next
to each other on the oldest sister's porch
in Dayton, Ohio. Each wears a sundress
as bright as their smiles fixed in place
for the camera.

I snapped the picture
that has now become proof of their existence.
Even then, I wondered if they were conscious
or semi-conscious that such a day might never
come again when they would all be together,
futures set in place, sun on their faces?

These women, unknowing each would die sometime
in the next ten years, liked to dance, drink and keep
neighbors at a distance, and, like the caterpillar in
Alice's Adventures in Wonderland, made their words
mean what they wanted them to mean.

I watched each of their lives dim and die,
and now, sometimes when I walk past the mantel,
I stop, study the black and white photo
behind a glass frame, see if I can remember
in what succession they passed. Before
I switch on a lamp, the picture disappears
as shadows do in too much light, and then
I turn and leave the room and them
with their perpetual poses and own kind
of permanence.

A HALLOWEEN POEM

The three-story, pre-Civil-War house creaks.
It's gray, unfinished clapboard sags.
Spider webs wreath its windows. In each,
a jack-o'-lantern flickers bright yellow.
Tombstones in the mouth of the neighboring
churchyard are moonlit teeth crooked as
arthritic hands. A picket fence encompasses
the house. Its jagged spears impale low
cumulus clouds that roll from a black sky.
Wind whips walls of leaves against
trick-or-treaters.

A man's silhouette, a bent branch, creeps
from street to bush, lunges from house
to house, staying only for seconds
in side yards. His bony, long fingers bear
a scythe. His ebony cape rides wind.
He is not in costume.
He is real as the everlasting.

When he approaches the three-story house,
his knock echoes to the cupola.
The door no one wants to answer squeaks open.
Only swirls of air greet him. He curses
at those who evade, who last longer
than he expected. He turns away.
The door slams shut, and he vanishes
like sleep in the morning.
The jack-o'-lanterns sneer.

THE HALLOWEEN PARTY

For a month, Mom and her sister, Mary,
planned a Halloween party for friends
in their eighth-grade class. They pocketed
their ten cents per day for lunch.

By the week of Halloween, they had saved
enough for crepe paper and jelly beans.
All through the girls' planning, their dad
remained silent, the epitome of nonchalance,
a weasel in a hole waiting to snap a chicken's
neck. His ears were shut to their talk.

In class, Freddie Schmidt, whose dad owned
Schmidt's Sausage, sat behind Mom, promised
to donate wieners and buns.

The day before the party, sisters strung crepe
paper streamers, filled dishes with jelly beans.

Halloween night, their dad lounged
in his recliner beneath orange and black
streamers. When he heard a knock at the door,
he barked, "I'll get it." He put his newspaper down,
ripped the door open. Freddy's arms balanced
boxes. Their dad huffed, "What do you want?"
A turtle retracting its head, Freddy answered,
"I've come to Dorothy's party." With his hand
on the doorknob, their dad blurted, "There's no party
here."

Next day at school, Freddie and classmates
sang a constant chorus of ridicule.
“How did you like Mary and Dorothy's party?
Wasn't it's swell?” For days, embarrassment
followed the girls around like a rabid dog,
while their father never spoke a word either way.

PART FOUR

CITY OF HAMMERS

As if engaged in pagan sacrifice,
his blood smears upon white piano keys.
All-day practice seven days a week,
mandated by his father, has weakened
Joel's interest in becoming a professional,
and on this particular day, caused his
fourteen-year-old fingers to bleed practicing
a sonata by Bela Bartok.

Neither parent is home.
His mom is at the hair salon, while
his father signs papers downtown
for the electric company's easement
on their property. Joel feels free to act
on impulse, trudges to the shed, unlocks it,
steps into dusky gloom. The sledgehammer
leans in the corner. He grabs work gloves
from a shelf, hauls the sledge into the house.

Late afternoon sun tinges piano keys
like smoke-stained fingers. Using
his entire body weight, the first blow collapses
the middle of the keyboard. Chips of ivory splay
in all directions like pieces of white fireworks
or an explosion of fingernails. He beats
the housing until it falls out of place exposing
hammers and strings. At the height of his anger,
he pounds down the row of hammers until
they collapse like dominoes. His sweaty hands
release the sledge. The ruined piano lies open
like a wooden wound. Joel's hands hurt, but
he is ready for his parents' rage. They will
come home to a boy much less broken now
than the piano itself.

ALONG THE BEACH

for Hart Crane

The broth of your grave washes ashore.
I kneel as if to dress in your skin, and
foam of your blood washes around
ankles. Conch shells catch you, hold you
little more than seconds it took your
helpless hunger to jump overboard.

Fields of the sun's flames burn
over the Gulf as I claw up water that
drains from my hands as quickly as death.
I pretend you had a perfect end, solved
the problem of too much desire
for poetry and pretty men.

You obviously did not want light
any longer, and though you did not drown
under silky stars, the morning you leapt
from the bridge, brightness of intention
gleamed upon the waves.

In a few seconds, you disappeared
like an ordinary man on an ordinary day,
hardness of air pushing you over
the lost edge of reconsideration.

HART CRANE WASHES ASHORE

Walking the beach this spring morning
at Litchfield, South Carolina, I imagine
your grave washed ashore. Air is fat
with sun boiling broth of your bones over
my bare feet. Foam of your blood swirls
around my ankles. Wherever water touches
me, I am dressed in your skin.

I kneel to scoop up an angel wing shell,
and you are there, burn of recognition
in my knees. Flames of seething sun claw
waves, make a silvery field silky as stars.

I pretend you had a perfect death,
drowned under noon sky without further
desire for light. Surf eddies around my feet
like lace of death. I dig toes into sand,
a part of the permanent coffin you stepped
into from the stern of the Orizaba
after you tossed your seaweed-colored coat
aside. Even deck crew couldn't hold you
in their arms to keep you from falling.

EDNA ST. VINCENT MILLAY IS DEAD

Her legs buckle at the top of the stairs.
Her heart, the timepiece of hell, stops.
She cannot watch the fall
because her mind is stone black.
Fingers no longer grasp air.
Her lifeless body jounces down each step
and crumples at the bottom in a drift
of blue nightgown and matching slippers.
For eight hours her broken beauty lies
undiscovered. The nearest neighbor lives
a mile away. She no longer hears owls hoot
in the Berkshire Hills or the scrape of
October's yellow leaves claw the window.
The key turns in the lock of the back door.
The caretaker, James Pinnie, enters
to start the evening fire. He ambles
down the hallway, turns the corner
into the foyer and discovers her face down.
He feels for the pulse, touches her
still pallid flesh. Shock of discovering her
beneath layers of silk compels him
to call the coroner. "Miss Millay is dead," he says
into the phone. "You mean the poet?" he hears
on the other end. "Yes. The poet."
The coroner arrives, lays his bowler on the side table,
bends into his pronouncement of finality.
The two men stand silent as they wait
for the undertaker and family to arrive.
A sudden ray of orange dawn spreads across
hardwood floor, stains the end of her
wealthy manners and luxurious decay.

THE RHYTHM OF SIN

She lives in the shadow of her parents'
teachings. From childhood to grown woman,
they fed her God's pitch for goodness,
and she swallowed all of it.

She has wed herself to chastity,
remote-control television,
and long telephone conversations,
carnal desire as suppressed as light
by a window blind. She only embraces
a mop, the handle of a lawn mower,
the solitude of books. Her goal is to qualify
as a ten on some fictitious, biblical scale.

Each night, she drops into the over-stuffed sanctuary
of a worn-out recliner, pulls her bathrobe tighter
against chill of seclusion.

Tonight, before bed, she parts drapes,
peeps out at October rain sparkling in the halo
of a streetlight. Fingers of water caress
the window, stream downward like cellophane,
jail bars.

Tonight, for seconds, she presses palms against glass.
The possibility of a lover shadows in beside her,
but she does not know how to strip herself
of convictions, to free herself from manufactured guilt.
Her flesh trembles. She draws back from the window.
She will not break God's back by allowing
even an imagined person to lay hands on her.

As if she has done something wrong,
she jerks drapes shut on denial,
boundless shame seeming to emanate
from a church to which she's never been.

THE SOMBER LIFE OF SUSAN BRIGHTLY

My neighbor greeted me at her door, mediocre
looks, a forty-five-year-old virgin who from birth
has been the first page of an unappealing and
unread book. I stepped inside, handed her
a valentine. It might have been ice-covered,
she was so hesitant between the reaching out
and the taking.

She had dated a man twenty-five years ago,
someone who had waited as patient as a deer
hunter for her to change her mind about sex.
She wouldn't relent, no matter how carefully
he broached the subject. Only after marriage
would she lose her purity, and if marriage
and sex didn't happen, she insisted
on taking her maidenhood to the grave
in a white dress. In the end, he doffed
his hat and left, telling her goodbye
across the emptiness of her life.
No man had ever mattered since or been
allowed to light up her eyes with promises.

She opened the valentine, laid it on the desk,
pulled her housecoat tighter around a protruding
stomach. I lowered into a folding chair, noted
the dilapidated couch, threadbare recliner
she slouched in daily to watch an outdated
TV set. She hoarded money, had more
than sufficient security. To my surprise,
she had once disclosed the amount. She kept
every sales slip she'd ever been given. I tried
to keep pity out of my conversations with her.

She offered me a glass of iced tea, extravagant
generosity I could count on during every visit.
I didn't dislike her. We talked much
on the phone which I once threw against
a cement block wall in the basement because
her narrow mind insisted everything
in the world came down to black or white
without the need for logic or analysis.

I sipped tea, certain as the stars her clay
would never be touched, certain if I gave
too much of myself, she would take a part
of me I do not want to give, and yet, I am
embarrassed by her singleness not just because
it separates her from most others, but
because it is mine, too.

AUTUMN PARLORS

You have not known love tender as a shiver
of wheat blown by a hint of breeze.
If I could, I would loosen you from years
of controlled hands, let them seek, reach,
clothe, and collapse deep within another
person's warmth. Yours is refined cruelty,
a frosted life self-imposed. Birds are all
that come near you, dancing stiffly, picking
at jewel-colored leaves like spinsters sorting
patterns of loneliness in their autumn parlors.

ANOTHER MAN

Slightly drunk, he swaggers to her bed,
hovers above her naked body. His flabby
torso repulses her, but tolerance is a tacit
part of the proposition.

He drools for the taste of her love. His sweat
drips onto hers and her conscious longing
to be with someone she desires. He grinds
into her passivity, moans over her minimal
response. She is apprehensive about
the unexpected. Six weeks ago, a truck
driver insisted on rough play, left rope burns
on her arms and legs.

He shrinks back a little, gazes at her.
Her mind drifts to a drawer and the gun
in it. She imagines shooting him
out of the rubble of her bed, but at that moment,
he lifts himself from her and fishes a cigarette
from the pack in his pants crumpled on the floor.
She rises too. He steps behind her, massaging
her shoulders while she rolls eyes upward
as if looking for sky.

Dressed, he hauls cash from his wallet,
jokingly tells her to keep the change, ignorant
she feels she's sold the magic-lantern show
of her soul.

LEAVING

She secures a hammerlock on God,
steers him out of her life.
On this mid-September afternoon,
she shuffles bare feet across gray, living
room carpet toward a wingback chair.
She has whispered this denunciation aloud.

Slumped in the chair, she tightens toes into soft,
yellow sunspots that lie on the carpet
like spilled egg yolk. She can no longer be
a woman who trumpets heaven and heaven's
authority. Those days have slipped away
much as her attention has from the pastor's
Sunday sermons, consciousness nearly fading
into sleep. As if anesthetized, she felt nothing
last time she attended church. Her faith,
like a loose petal from its stem,
has broken free of any creed.

She sips Merlot that blurs her
body, quiets flux of doubt.
Yet, she feels vulnerable as a dry leaf
on a flame to be left with only
brutal parchment on which is written
loneliness and solidarity.

The room belongs to silence.
Eyes closed, she rests her head
against the back of the chair,
obliterates thought, so as not to see
what is left of her brittle beliefs.

HAYDEN'S FAILURE

His name was George Hayden, my cousin,
but most called him Hayden. I remember
the day I saw him stumbling out of the bar
across the street from where I lived.
He beckoned me over, begged for help.
I drove him to a local hospital where he stayed
for two months until he dried out.

He moved in with me on his release from rehab.
Divorced, his only child deceased, he had no
responsibilities but himself. He attended AA
meetings faithfully, stayed sober for thirty-seven
years, then one night he grabbed his car keys,
as if they would disappear any minute, and barked
You can say whatever you think you need to say
to save me. Just don't stand in the way
of my first drink tonight.

I trailed him out the door,
slung myself into the passenger seat and pleaded
let me talk to you. There are things
we can do to prevent this. He was about to wear
clean clothes to play in the mud, and would
come away with irremovable stains. He wouldn't
respond, clinched his jaw, floored the accelerator.
During the surreal ride, I saw trees, houses, streets
blur into a stream of hopelessness.
What triggered this? I shouted. *You're*
throwing away years of sobriety.
His neck stiffened, and he whipped the Chevy
Camaro into the parking lot of Berlin's Carry-Out.
I could do nothing but race along behind him.
Ironically, the place was ready to close, but
we made it through the door in time for a final sale.
He ordered a case of Bud Light, a quart of Jack Daniels'.

On the way home I sat quiet as a windless day.
He drove hard, gripping the wheel as if
it would be torn away from him at any moment.
I tried to reason, but he was beyond reason
as if I were talking to a high diver
who was in the middle of the dive.

Two years later, he died
of Cirrhosis of the liver, the cumulative effect
of previous years of drinking precipitated
by his relapse. The obituary read:
His name was George Hayden,
but most called him Hayden.

CLOUD MOTEL

She dives under gloss of waves, tangles
in yellow webs of surface sun, stands
in waist high water. Streams of the Atlantic
drain from dazzling shoulders. When she
reaches shore, her weightless shadow
seeks balance, blinks a blinding look upward
where seagulls scratch blue marks
on a square of sky. Neck snaked up, she stares
at cumulus clouds that have shaped
into a motel room like the one last night
in which an admirer charmed her out of secrets.
No doubt, she will not see him again,
a traveling man bent on a new location.
Yet, it wasn't a seduction. They had bargained
for each other.

Shreds of last night stick to her skin like sand
on the bottom of her feet. Tonight, she will not
hang at Burman's Bar. She will return
to watch the sea churn a broken moon,
to see the silk of evening make a safe path
of light to shore, and she will sleep satisfied
to be beyond the hunger of a man's way.
Her door will be closed to self-serving passion.
She will lie down alone, doorway within reach
of the sea, breasts only as warm as her own breath.

DOROTHY

She twisted more than a million miles
into brooding sky, unhinged from home.
Chicken feathers and Kansas heat disappeared
behind her, and that was after Toto jumped
into sunlight, coated with sudden dust from
wicked bicycle wheels.

These were the terms that summer day
when the world reeled away without politeness,
and a shaft of black cloud flung her bed
from wall to wall. Even stones flew fast enough
to melt out of existence.

Oh, Dorothy, did you ever know
how hard you came down into that moment
of impeccable surprise, your house
suddenly in shiny Technicolor, your family left
with the predicament of how to get you home
and you being there all the time?

What would you do to go back to Oz again,
to see overlarge flowers, small, luminous faces,
and your three fellow travelers?

Are you happy back here on earth where
hope often falls into the rain gutter
along with regret that you ever returned?

RUSTLER'S COMMENT

Jack faces a saloon mirror,
slings a look at a stranger who glances
back. Soon, the stranger stares at Jack,
as if inviting a challenge. Jack slugs
his whiskey, slaps a coin down on the bar,
squeezes callused fingers into a fist of rage.
Feeling his manhood has been questioned,
he slides from the wooden stool, anger,
a flashing glint, as he locks eyes
with the other man. Nonchalant, Jack
flicks cigarette ash to the floor. He is
a cattle rustler who occasionally splashes
across river or stream with a herd
of stolen shadows. Now, however, he
hangs his head just enough to shade
his face. When he passes behind
the stranger, Jack pats his holster,
warning wrapped in a twitch of lip,
and pushes through the swinging doors.

Jack unhitches his horse. Sweat
on his forehead quivers down his nose.
Without looking, he senses someone
beside him. They spur their steeds
in the ribs, bolt out of town.

It is early noon. Sun is tequila yellow.
They rein in their horses under an old elm
bordering miles of cornfield. The men
dismount, unholster their guns and shoot
near each other's feet. Their laugh is
just enough to bring relief from pretentious
moments. Jack reaches out, holds
the stranger tight against the sway
of his own weight. The kiss is an
exclamation point confirming
mutual desire, the necessary quiet
without which there wouldn't be
enough rope to hang them both.

THE RELIGION OF JIM BARRINGTON'S HAIRCUT

Jim picked his Afro into a brown halo
of perfection, every hair
in a preconceived place.
Caught without an umbrella, on days
when wind or rain threatened to
disturb his mammoth bouffant,
he would dart from shelter to shelter
like a thief protecting stolen goods.

He hid forty years of self-doubt beneath
coiffed extremism. His hair looked
manufactured, as if in adherence
to an 11th commandment: thou shalt
wear flawless hair.

The change occurred while watching
rain pebble a window. Jim pressed so
close to the glass his hair disappeared
from reflection, leaving only his
face, a luminous bone of light.
Slowly, he backed away,
realization storming his mind fast
as fishing line jerked with a catch.
He wouldn't hide under hair anymore.
The pick lay on a dresser. He tossed pick
and indecision into a wastebasket.

The barber launched her scissors
into a hundred small snips, working
from section to section. Jim's head
emerged with the close cut he hadn't
had since teenage years.

Driving home, he let wind whip through
the open window, raked a hand over
freedom from compulsion
and the crown of his buzzed head.

UNDRESSING THE PRIEST

I watch you each Sunday morning, back stiff
as the crucifix nailed to the wall above
your head. When you turn around to face
the Bible, elevated on a mahogany lectern,
I focus on your perfect fingers turning pages
toward redemption. Your commitment appears
impeccable, incapable of sin, but the kiss
before you left our house was not a dream
kiss. It was as real as the black suit
you insisted on wearing as if dressing
for the grave.

I have tried to help you slip out of your fear
of discovery that fits you like a too-tight
shirt, elbows snagged in armholes of guilt,
face smothering against The Rite of Ordination.
I have begged you to burn the cloth, free yourself
to wear nakedness against me,
but duplicity continues to rub your heart raw.

Your shadow leans over the lectern. Your beautiful
hands do not turn another page, satisfied
it seems to belong to a charade of devotion.

POSE

He smokes his first cigarette to strike
a cocky stance. To pass time, he leans
against a wall in an adult theater.
He slouches, reluctant to stand too straight,
maintains the macho effect. His lips
pout smoke, as if it is even possible
to shape smoke rings from amateurish puffs.

The theater is dimly lit. Dampness
has tormented paint from walls. Strips
the size of a human hand hang loose.
Men parade a well-worn path up and down
aisles, through the lobby to the restroom,
come back out, start again. A constant
procession of desperate faces passes him.
He stands still watching, waiting for someone
to stop with a come-on line or a roving hand.
Amidst smoke and gloom, most faces appear
gray as corpses, seem bent on not showing
an interest in each other. His eyes don't lock
on anyone for fear of dispelling detached appeal.

Propped against a wall, in his silence he dreams
of another way to look at the universe
that doesn't lead here. Eyes averted, he thinks
there must be more to do than loiter here
with a sneer fixed to his face as if with glue.
He and the others never smile. To do that
would violate caution and watchfulness.

So, what did hanging along these walls mean,
the risk of arrest always imminent?
He can only say that for a while the cigarette
and pretense let him become someone else,
let him get into the world the only way he knew how.

Back home, safe from apprehension,
he tries to love the part of himself he saved back,
not squandered during leather-jacketed hours
being cautious, loitering in shadows to hide
his flaccid neck and the top of his fading hair.

PART FIVE

PROPHET OF DECEMBER DUSK

Dimitar brushes
a cold look
onto everything,
caresses the skin
of dusk with less
light, heaps snow
onto shimmering
branches. Faces
partly hidden
within turned up collars,
we walk against welts
of drunken winds,
round a corner
and a whip of old
leaves whirl
against horizon,
a fistful of the end
of autumn lingering
in its late hours
like these
midnight walks
we take toward home.
In the country,
God is a twig,
a vein
of eventual twilight,
someone banking snow
against the front door.

FROM A RENTED CABIN AT LAKE ERIE

Gulls graze shoreline. Morning sun, intense
as an open, red wound, inches above horizon.
Some gulls stand still as lawn ornaments, then,
in a single spasm, glide into sky
above the ripple of harbor fish.
I have seldom seen such passion. It may be
worth giving up my body to become one of these birds,
their gray-white bellies the color of the lake.
I strip to the waist, stand idle as a hunter,
shirt flung over a tan shoulder.
My bare feet traipse through swaying grasses
to the front steps.

The rest of the day, everything seems
all right, even getting older and closer
to the corner around which when I turn,
I will no longer be.

Eventually, sunset drags daylight out of sight.
I drop onto the bed, ebb into sleep.

Tomorrow, a flame of morning will sketch
shore birds into existence, and I will follow them,
arms at my sides, my desire to fly
no different than theirs.

INTRUDER

A boot
is too big
to fit
into these woods
without crushing
flower heads.

It crackles
over the butterfly's thorax
with a slap
of leather,
smears wing color,
a tissue-thin layer
of wasted rainbow.

REQUIEM FOR A RED MAPLE

Like an arm rising from the ground,
the trunk, strong as muscle, branches
upward sprouting hundreds of limbs.
Each leaf suspends on sporadic breezes.
Each leaf a surrender to red, glints
imperfect glimmers of sunlight.

Leaves, the size of a human hand, loosen,
and, like a human life, let go.
Even on a day burnished with an astonishment
of blue sky, they curl into pseudo fists, fall
against each other's defeat on their way
to the ground.

I have lived through this before, wanting
the dead not to be dead, to stay attached.
I want to sit at a breakfast table, turn toward
a window, see leaves unfurling, flying back
to the tree like a movie in reverse,
leaves flying upwards to bare branches,
banishing October burial.

SNOW ON THE GRASS OF APRIL

The first days of unpredictable April turns its
sack of tricks upside down, empties its contents
of cold winds and a smattering of snowflakes,
small enough to have fallen from a giant
salt shaker, upon the village of Dedham.
It's spring's sleight of hand powdering lawns
with remnants of winter that disappear in seconds,
a reminder not to pencil in warm weather too soon.
Nevertheless, a hint of cloud-white blossoms
has surfaced on magnolia trees, and shoots
of hyacinths have pushed through hard soil.

I think twice about days by a steady fire,
windows frosted with lacy designs,
the dogwood bowed in gowns of ice.
I don't know if I'm ready to be released
from winter's raw embrace, its remembered rap
of wind on the windows and how it held me
cloistered in long nights and early lamplight.
During winter, I mellowed into solitude.
Now, it is a kind of loss to account for as
sun brightens creeks and streams, and branches
puff out pink blooms.

Another April I live alone, become a hound pulling
at his leash of isolation, longing for a pairing
of the heart.

THE CHURCHYARD TREE

The churchyard tree is greening out
this seventh day of May. Five different
trunks twist into one monstrous braid.
Limbs fountain up, curve back
almost forming perfect circles.
It is a deformed tree. That is its beauty.
There will be nothing like its misshapen reach
into the lower part of the sky. Telephone wires
and cables run through it, marring its singularity.

Dusk dims daylight to a smear of gloom.
The truth of predicted rain falls quick
and silent like the dogwood blossoms.
A tease of thunder sounds far away
as the next county but belongs to mine.

The tree, the tree, ugly as lies,
mangles out of the earth
like God's inaccurate guess
at what a tree should look like.

THE ARTIST OBSERVES A DEAD TREE

Five separate offshoots of one tree trunk twist
into each other. It looks as if a giant has braided
the limbs together into one gnarled distortion.
Nothing is more naked than barren limbs
when everything understood about a tree is dead.
What illness killed the annual rings, or was it
stone-cold nothing of old age that stripped it bare?
There will be no more listening to language
of restless leaves. Maybe somewhere its heart
still struggles. As the psychology book says,
everything has a psyche.

Someday, someone will paint, sculpt, or photograph it
because it is misshaped, malformed, and gnarled.
Some people hunger for the ugly, enjoy breathing
dark thoughts and even adore the deterioration of stars.

This tree is nothing now but a rupture in the earth
from which birds still speak echoes. This tree
represents impeccable death, wrapped in the question
of what it is still doing here? Someday, an artist,
swayed by appreciation, sympathy, or regret, will paint
this tree that has poked a hole in heaven from which
a surprise of butterflies will pour out of the opening.

HORNETS

Michael always had a little more interest
in science than the other students. So,
it wasn't a surprise when he carried
a hornet's nest into the classroom
for everyone to examine.
It lay there a short time before
a hornet crawled out the end.
Fearing hornets would swarm
the classroom, he sped out
the door to the other science teacher
across the hall to ask for help, but
he was on break. Worse, Michael's
teacher had been summoned to the phone
in the office. One by one, hornets
fled their nest. Michael found a can
of wasp spray in the cupboard, a spray
used in autumn when wasps flew through
the school's open windows. He aimed the can,
and the unbelievable happened. The hornets
transformed into human facsimiles.
One stepped forward and spoke:
If you kill us, you will destroy something
valuable, something desired by the whole world.
We can offer you peace. You rant, pontificate,
send righteous greeting cards about peace
on earth at Christmas, but when peace comes
to you, you want to fight, exterminate, kill it.

We can give you an opportunity
never before presented to the human race,
the secret to everlasting peace.
What's the catch? The catch is
you have to join us, become a hornet,
one of us. Another student, Brandon,
shouted *Never! We don't want to be*
trapped in a hornet's body forever.
We like who we are! Give me that can!
We'll get rid of you and that will be that!

In the meantime, more hornets escaped
the nest and transformed. Their shadowy figures
overwhelmed the room. Michael raced
to one of the lab cupboards, grabbed
chloroform, doused the face of the anthropoid
who had just spoken. It's features shriveled.
Its body withered to the floor.
The rest of the students egged Michael on.
One by one the pseudo-humans shrank into their
original form and died. Students swept
the insects into a pile and put the pile into the trash.
Michael kept the nest as a souvenir
of conquest and as a reminder of the day
he and friends rescued themselves
from a spurious proposition.

THERE IS A WAY OF NOT NOTICING GOD

There is a way of not noticing God
as abrupt as ice or short, cold touches.
I just believe, resolved through inference,
and yet shrugged off like useless coats against
diverse lies, contradictory sentiments.
Skeptical belief is the best reprieve.

Not looking for solace or a reprieve,
the smear of sunlight mistaken for God
has often affected men's sentiments.

MATCHSTICK

The flame,
in blue and yellow dress,
wobbles
like a wounded dancer.

Cruelty of time
or a breath
dims its performance
to a frantic flicker
that fades to dark
without celebration
or the burn
of applause.

THE LIMITS OF SYMPATHY

You slow down breathing, speak
in whispers. Your doctor gives you three weeks.
I lean forward, intent on feeling
your emotions. You recite preparations
for the encroachment of death. Before you finish,
I dare a sideways glance at the clock;
hope you do not see me, careful to return my eyes
to pain in yours. You keep talking.
I look at the floor. I expect silence, but
figure talking must keep you from fright.
When you run out of words, your face
is expressionless. I slump, full of defeat,
and want to leave the room.

I drive home, tell myself the lie,
I've done all I can.
What should I have said to a person
who can not fit into life anymore?

WHEN POETRY DISAPPEARS

When I had been seriously ill
from a heart attack and dehydration,
I didn't write poems or breath poetry.
That surprised me because I didn't think
anything but death could separate me
from writing. Mom used to say if you don't
have good health, you don't have anything.

Before emergency, bypass surgery,
blackness flooded my brain.
I slipped into non-language mode
dominated by fever. I saw space
in my head the color of salt.
No particular image materialized,
just a milky nothing.

As I lay in the hospital bed,
priorities jumped into place.
I wanted poetry to be bigger
than bad health. When my heart sagged
toward the end, words ceased to exist.
I disbelieved the same blood
pulsed in my body that once throbbed
with the need to write all night.

With every shift toward recovery, poetry
surfaced again as my prime consideration.
Back at my desk, gentler health allows me
to write this. I wish I had found the answer
to serving poetry while on a sick bed,
to quiet my mind from shouting for it.

PART SIX

HAVE YOU TRIED MURDER IN DECEMBER?

She had often thought of killing him,
but it was December, the time for joy.
Yet, as she sat in the brown, leather,
swivel chair in the study, she couldn't
help but to focus on the paper weight.
It would be convenient to pound
a couple thuds into a skull, but the mess
would be unacceptable.

What about a fall in the kitchen,
his head striking the microwave,
ripping a gap from which would flow
final blood?

She plotted while she stacked newspapers,
ran the sweeper. Winding cord around
sweeper hooks, she thought about a noose,
it's efficacy and cleanliness. There would be
no untidiness, just a moment of good riddance.

He would never agree to divorce.
A sycophant husband, a cowed servant
he went along with her pantomime
of a perfect marriage.

He had never caught her cheating.
She was good at hiding it beneath a veneer
of tepid affection and regular cookouts
with the neighbors. Her lover was twenty
years younger than she, and had Gary's red hair,
knocked back a six-pack per day as a cure
for heroin withdrawal. She loved him with ardor
because he bought her trinkets and didn't mind
her wrinkled hands. Well, these hands would
soon be busy clearing the way for the younger man.

She had never dabbled in poison.
That was a possibility, too.
On the other hand, her husband had suffered
a number of recent falls, once in the kitchen
and once near the basement steps. Of course.
That was the answer. She would give
his doddering self a little push to help him
toward his workshop in the basement.

When the day arrived, she dusted
furniture, unfroze the evening meal.
As usual, after dinner, he headed to his workshop.
She sneaked up behind him, and in the instant
when he felt her touch, grabbed her arm,
and they both tumbled down the steps.

She lay below the last step with a fractured skull,
the gaunt look of death, a gray mask upon her face.
He suffered a knee injury and a broken hip
which pinned him in a wheelchair.

DISGRUNTLED ROADWORK

Seven men in orange and yellow vests
stand close together forming a clump
of testosterone. Men number eight and nine
hold poles with *stop* on one side
and *slow* on the other. The work area
includes two city blocks. A pole man
at either end coordinates their signs,
so traffic through the work area can be
stopped or warned to drive slowly.

I approach the blocked zone.
Man number eight flips his sign around
to read *slow.* I obey, inch my car through
the first block into the second.
Man number nine, on closer observation,
is actually a blonde woman with curls
tucked under a hard hat. Her sign says *stop*
instead of *slow*. Traffic behind me brakes
to a standstill. Horns blare. I slump
lower in my seat, wondering why number nine
hasn't flipped her sign instead of her mind.
Behind me, impatient drivers continue tooting.

A woman with big hair and a chihuahua
draped over her arm, like a four-legged bracelet,
leaps from a Hyundai, shrieks *what the hell's
going on?* The dog's bulgy eyes water.
Its ears twitch like antennae picking up
every word of the woman's obscenities.

Just as the cacophony of horns begins
to shred my eardrums, the blonde looks
at her sign, turns red, and flips it
to the *slow* side.

Back in gear, I pass her, thinking they should
pack all nine of the laborers into a porta potty
and rocket it to the moon.

LICENSE LUNACY

It's time to renew my driver's license.
The Ohio Bureau of Motor Vehicles,
also known as the Odd Lots of people,
opens its doors at 8 a.m., and I'm there
at 7:30. Already, the line is as long
as the Arabian peninsula. 1,256,000 people
idle outside. I'm number 1,256,001.

Doors open on a staff of dour faces
and dispositions that make lion trainers
look like ninnies. Clerks await the onslaught
of beings who range from a coiffed diva,
whose Clive Christian No.1 lmperial Majesty
perfume wafts its $205,000 scent past me,
to a malodorous man who has apparently
placed a moratorium on soap.

A millennium later, it's my turn.
I retrieve necessary identification
from my briefcase: a social security card,
birth certificate, two pieces of validation
to prove residency, most recent
colonoscopy results, parents' death
certificates, genealogy charts
for each side of my parents' family
going back to the year 936,
gun carrying permit, baby footprint,
and the accompanying nude shot,
high school grade cards, bank statements
for the year, charts for diet plans
I may have tried, and results of any strip search
I have undergone.

The worker stamps OK on my forehead,
thumbs me to her right where I sit down
in front of a camera. I look at my new license,
try not to see the picture of myself, but masochism
sneaks a peek of Quasimodo after a hurricane.
At the risk of trying her patience, I ask for a marker
and a piece of paper. She begrudgingly hands
the items to me as if I had asked for her purse.
I quickly print, leave the building,
march to my car and place the "For Sale" sign
under a windshield wiper.

MISSING MONEY

My birthday is April first, so it’s hard
to resist pranks. The first phone call
to my parents announced I had lost
money they had given me that evening
for my birthday. The hunt began.
They tossed living room cushions,
peered under bushes, looked in places
I didn't even know existed. A call
back to me announced they had not found
the money. I said I was sure I had lost it
at their place, so the hunt continued.
Numerous calls back and forth
reported futile results. A hundred dollars
is not a large sum of money, but
it was a gift and that made it valuable.
I pleaded with them to continue to look.
I knew it was somewhere in their house.
They returned to couch cushions and bushes.
On the next call, I asked if they had
searched the driveway. Maybe it had dropped
out of my pocket when I bent into my car.
Yes, I had searched my car. It wasn't there.
When tension built to its highest point,
I made a last call and shouted, “April fool!”
Mom shouted back, “April fool.”
We knew you hadn't lost it.
Your brother saw you jam the money
into your jean’s pocket. We realized after
the first call what you were pulling.
We faked our searches. This year,
the joke is on you.

WHAT IS THE LATIN WORD FOR CAKE?

The day before Mom's birthday, I decided
to bake her a cake. I retrieved Betty Crocker's
cookbook and began. An important Latin test
scheduled for the next day didn't stop me
from shoving ingredients into the oven.
I was way behind in my Latin lessons.
Not only did I have to study for a big test,
but I had to peruse numerous chapters.
I felt tired, lay on the bed with my Latin
book propped up on my chest and fell asleep.

Around two in the morning, I awoke,
terrified I'd burned down the house.
I flew to the kitchen, jerked the oven
door open. The cake wasn't even done!
I had set the temperature to 350.
I didn't understand why the cake wasn't baked.
I went back to bed with my Latin book
and fell asleep again. At seven in the morning,
I startled awake, knew for sure this time
there would be a black hole where the kitchen
used to be. I sprang from bed, raced to the oven.
The cake was a golden brown.

I'll never know why it took so long to bake.
The oven must not have heated up to 350,
or maybe my guardian angel hovered over the stove.
I don't know the answer. I only know I got a D
on the Latin test and gave myself an A
for the cake, an A for amazing.

HAPPY HOARDERS

Two friends of mine, Henry and Pete, abhor
space, not astronomical space but space
in closets, cupboards, and refrigerators.
Something about emptiness threatens
them because they keep those spaces filled
to the brim. Both of them have a compulsion
to shop and bring home everything
they can carry. When Henry comes to visit,
he always leads the way with numerous bags
of groceries and purchases from the thrift
store. He has eliminated every space
in my house, including the basement.
Henry is currently double layering
by stacking things upon things.
No two men are more generous than
these two, and perhaps it all started
because they were born in a U-Haul truck.
I know no other explanation for their urge
to collect. They seem satisfied to own
items per se.

On the other hand, my mom was spare
about everything. She kept nothing
that didn't serve a logical, practical,
and immediate purpose. In fact.
if I came into her house and hung my coat
on the back of a chair, twenty minutes later,
the coat disappeared, forever. She didn't like
clutter, valued space. In every house
she owned, she knocked out walls
to make areas more spacious. Her influence
makes me think the ideal house would be
one with freshly painted rooms, new carpet,
and no furniture.

I love space as much as Henry and Pete
love cramming it to overflow. For their
next birthdays, I'm planning to buy each
of them either a backhoe or a steam shovel.

FUDGED

On a snowy, blowy, January afternoon,
Mom allowed me to traipse into the kitchen
while she cooked. Typically, I was not
allowed to bother her when she cooked,
but this afternoon, she was making fudge
and said I could help. The alternative
of going outside, however warm coat
and hat, did not appeal as much as helping
her make fudge.

She added ingredients into an oversized pan.
When contents were ready to heat, I stirred
with the admonition not to stop
because the fudge would burn.
Chocolate fudge sounded delicious.
I couldn't wait to have a piece. She took over,
finished by whipping butter into the brown mass.
Then, she poured it all into a glass, baking dish.
I ate what was left in the pan. Within the next
half hour, the fudge began to harden and harden
and harden. We tried to cut it, but it broke
the knife blade. We couldn't get it out of the dish.
Mom said to fetch a screwdriver and a hammer.
The fudge wouldn't budge. Mom announced
We'd lost our place in the Anthony Thomas Hall
of Fame. She decided to soak the dish in water
overnight. At this point, she was only trying
to retrieve the dish.

Next morning, the fudge remained irretrievable.
We had no alternative but to throw away
the whole works. In despair, we talked seriously
about notifying the Anderson Concrete company
to see if they wanted to buy Mom's recipe.

ROACH RAGE

I taught in a high school replete with roaches,
not just the kind you smoke but six-legged
ones. The school was built in 1926, enough
time lapse for a sizable infestation to enroll.

One particular day stands out when
I saw a roach, as big as a Milky Way
candy bar, crawling across the front
of my classroom. My students spied it
too, and John Wiser, seated in the front,
sprang from his seat and tromped
the creature with his sneaker, but
the roach continued on toward the hallway.
In the next two seconds, half a dozen
other boys leapt from their seats, attempting
to smash the bug. It looked like a clogging
competition with everybody stomping feet.
Nobody succeeded in eliminating the invader,
and the roach continued toward the hallway.

At this point, an assistant principal came
sauntering in the same direction the roach
was traveling and, with his size fourteen shoe,
flattened the bug into oblivion.

Later that day, during my break, the school
librarian motioned me to her backroom.
On the countertop, around the sink, hundreds
of baby roaches scurried in every direction.
I'd never seen so many in one spot, didn't know
they came so small. Every roach I'd ever seen
in the building measured at least three inches long.

Extermination had only ever offered a temporary
solution.

I used to hang my coat on the open closet door
in my room, so that nothing would creep
into my pockets during the day. There were
certainly more roaches in the building than students,
and because the roaches constantly outmaneuvered us,
we teachers assumed the main difference between
the students and the insects was that the roaches had
higher SAT scores.

About the author

R. Nikolas Macioci earned a PhD from The Ohio State University, and for thirty years taught for the Columbus City Schools. In addition to English, he taught Drama and developed a Writers Seminar for select students. OCTELA, the Ohio Council of Teachers of English, named Nik Macioci the best secondary English teacher in the state of Ohio.

Nik is the author of two chapbooks:

- Cafes of Childhood and Greatest Hits

as well as fourteen other books:

- Why Dance?
- Necessary Windows
- Cafes of Childhood (original with additional poems)
- Mother Goosed
- Occasional Heaven
- A Human Saloon
- Rustle Rustle Thump Thump
- Rough
- The Melancholy Life of Doris Menning
- Stoney Seasons
- A Feast of Losses
- Gods of Disharmony
- The Only Country I've Been Dead In
- Dark Guitar

Critics and judges called *Cafes of Childhood* a "beautifully harrowing account of child abuse," but not "sentimental" or "self-pitying," an "amazing book," and "a single unified whole." *Cafes of Childhood* was submitted for the Pulitzer Prize in 1992. In addition, more than two hundred of his poems have been published here and abroad in magazines and journals, including *Chiron Review, Concho River Review, The Bombay Review, The Raven's Perch, The Main Street Rag, and West Trade Review*

He won First Place in the 1987 National Writers' Union Poetry Competition, judged by Denise Levertov, First Place in The Baudelaire Award Competition, sponsored by The World Order of Narrative and Formalist Poets (1989), Second Place in *Zone 3*'s first annual Rainmaker Awards, judged by Howard Nemerov (1989), and Second Place in the *Writer's Digest* annual competition, judged by Diane Wakoski (1991). In 2021, he was nominated for a Pushcart Prize and a Best of the Net award. In 2022, he was nominated for a Pushcart Prize. He was nominated for a Best of the Net award for 2023

Acknowledgements

Grateful acknowledgment is made to the following publications in which some of these poems first appeared:

"Carpet Stretchers" *The Ravensperch*
"Snow Hands" *The Ravensperch*
"Spring Story" *The Ravensperch*
"The Alzheimer's House" *The Ravensperch*
"The Rhythm of Sin" *The Ravensperch*
"Asphalt Memories" *The Ravensperch*
"A Journey Away from Tiresome Elegance" *The Ravensperch*
"How Sad the Young Lies Hurt" *The Ravensperch*
"A Halloween Poem" *Pink Plastic House*
"Inevitable Portrait" *The Rockford Review*
"Halloween Self Burial" *Stickman Review*
"Pickup" *Stickman Review*
"Edna St. Vincent Millay Is Dead' *The Big Windows Review*
"Snow on the Grass of April" *Euonia Review*
"Clothesline" *The Bangalore Review*

"Nothing More" *Red Ogre Review*
"Hornets" *Primeval Monster Zine*
"The Artist Observes a Dead Tree" *Sparks of Calliope*
"Crossing the Swiss Alps" *Door is A Jar*
"After Aunt Liz's Death" *Door is A Jar*
"Pose" The Raven's Perch
"Aunt Ada's Apples" The Raven's Perch
"Mammoth Hot Springs, Wyoming" The Raven's Perch
"All That We Never Said" The Raven's Perch

www.ingramcontent.com/pod-product-compliance
Lightning Source LLC
Chambersburg PA
CBHW070629310726
48982CB00001B/215
9798218203894